THE IRISH GORDON BENNETT CUP RACE 1903
# TRIUMPH OF THE RED DEVIL

ALSO BY BRENDAN LYNCH

*Green Dust — Ireland's Unique Motor Racing History 1900–1939*

*'A gentleman outside the car, a devil in it!'*
*Red Devil, Camille Jenatzy.*

THE IRISH GORDON BENNETT CUP RACE 1903

# Triumph of the Red Devil

Brendan Lynch

PORTOBELLO PUBLISHING

Published in 2002 by

Portobello Publishing
5 Middle Mountjoy Street
Dublin 7

© 2002 Brendan Lynch

All rights reserved. No part of this publication may be reproduced or utilised in any form or by any means digital, electronic or mechanical including photography, filming, video recording, photocopying, or by any information storage and retrieval system or shall not, by way of trade or otherwise, be lent, resold or otherwise circulated in any form of binding or cover other than that in which it is published without prior permission in writing from the publisher.

The publisher has made every effort to contact the copyright holders of text and illustrative material reproduced in this book. If any involuntary infringement of copyright has occurred sincere apologies are offered and the owners of such copyright are requested to contact the publisher.

ISBN 0-9513668-1-5

5 4 3 2 1

Cover design: David Houlden
Book design and typesetting: David Houlden
Printed by Betaprint

*To three late unforgettable friends:*

architect, Peter Stevens

artist, Owen Walsh

and

'Professor' Jimmy O'Donovan

*Ireland welcomes the racers.*

Published with assistance from the Society of the Irish Motor Industry, and Motor Distributors Limited, Irish Importers of Mercedes Cars.

# Acknowledgements

Many thanks to the SIMI and to Motor Distributors Limited for their generous support. Particularly to Cyril McHugh, President of the SIMI and his council members, and to Matt Fagan, Chairman of Motor Distributors Limited, importers of Mercedes cars to Ireland.

The unstinted support of Irish Vintage and Veteran Car Club President, Denis Dowdall was a major encouragement. Money does not buy such enthusiasm.

'I am already trying to fit twenty five hours into twenty four,' Sir Stirling Moss said recently. All the more reason to thank the last of the great drivers of a later heroic age for his time in perusing these pages and adding his generous Foreword. A gentleman and sportsman in the mould of Baron de Caters and Rene de Knyff. Thanks also to Lady Susan!

Also much appreciated are the interest and photographs of Guy de Caters, grandson of the sporting Baron de Caters. Appeals for sponsorship fared like my Christmas cards — many went out, few returned! A particular thanks, therefore, to Castrol's Gordon Elder and Paul Flanagan, Ann Stevens and the Leinster Motor Club, Neil Perry and Perry Motors of Athy, and Bertha Mulvey of KELT (Kildare European Leader II Teoranta).

Thanks to Dr. Noel Kissane, Keeper of Manuscripts of the National Library for his assistance with photographs and manuscript suggestions. Also to author Robert Dick, for his invaluable information on drivers' mechanics. And, particularly, to writer and ace proof-reader Adrian Kenny; motorsport artists Terry Ballance and Jim Cullen B.Eng.; photographer Arthur Browne; artist and writer, Brian Lalor; AIB's Don McClenahan; Bord Fáilte's John Brown and Captain Theo Ryan and Royal Irish Automobile Club President, Wilfie Fitzsimmons, for their interest and assistance.

As usual, the staff of the reading rooms of the National Library, Dublin, the British Library, London, the British Newspaper Library in Colindale, Trinity College Libraries and the Ilac Centre reference library were unfailingly patient, courteous and attentive.

*Autocar*'s Patrick Fuller and Simon Fox generously permitted the use of important photographs and the memorable illustration by Frederick Gordon-Crosbie. As did the speedy Mercedes archive staff in Stuttgart, DaimlerChrysler's Stan Peschel, Dieter Ritter, Maria Feifel and Maria Seisel.

I am indebted for further photos to Denis Dowdall; Dunlop's (UK) Judith Bodenham; Castrol's Vanna Skella; Dublin's National Library; Mme Thiriet of the Automobile Club de France; Michael Cooper; J.C. Persey; Tony Byrne; Con Costello and the History and Family Research centre at Kildare Co. Library; Marcus Klippgen, Dietrich Kuhlgatz and Charlotte Moisson of Bosch; and John Cooney for the marvellous Speed Trials photos taken by his grandfather John C. Cooney, winner of Ireland's first motorsport event.

Thanks for their prompt assistance to fellow Guild of Motoring Writers members Nick Georgano Graham Gauld, Tony Dron, David Burgess-Wise, John Blunsden, Dimitri Urbain and Halwart Schrader.

Also to Mario Corrigan, Local Studies Dept., Kildare History and Family Research Centre, Newbridge; Margaret O'Riordan, Athy Cultural centre; SIMI's Brian Cooke; Gordon Bennett descendants Hugh and Peter Newell; Ian Keers, Mercedes Club of Great Britain; Mike Treacy, Menoshire Book Distributors; Sean, Gary and Conri of Reads super copying service; Reg Plunkett and Norman Williams; John Dowling of Dowling's Pub (so convenient to Ballyshannon!); and Sam Hendy and Robert Hutton of Tippeenan.

And in Cebu, Philippines, thanks to Sir Jun and Rennillen, Kenneth of Century Hotel, and all at Pete's Kitchen and the Colonnade Youth Zone Computer Centre. Also to Alex Sinclair and Jacqui Breathnach of the RIAC; Jacques Deneef of the Belgian Automobile Club; Sue Hudson of DaimlerChrysler UK; Mr K.J. Sagar, First Secretary Indian Embassy, Dublin; Peadar and Treasa MacManus for translation services; Kieran White and Sean Cleary, chairman of The Gordon Bennett Company Ltd.; and Johnny and Mrs. Thomas, proud owners of Selwyn Edge's 1902 race-winning car!

I cannot let this book roll without paying tribute to other life-enhancing friends and acquaintances who are, sadly, are no longer around: Peter Stevens, Owen Walsh, Jimmy O'Donovan (who appreciated a good launch!), Patrick Ruth, Mrs. Andrews, and my parents Siobhan and Patrick Lynch. Also Michael Hartnett, Nevill Johnson, Joe Christle, the irrepressible Eamonn MacThomais, outstanding fellow-scribes David Hodges, Russell Bulgin, Ted Bonner and Portlaoise's Donal White, virtuoso driver Charles Martin and his wife, Joy, and Dublin racer David Manley.

Friends whose encouragement has been a consistent source of strength at delicate moments are John and Dymphna McMahon; Brendan and Frances Gallagher; artists Noel and Dymphna Lewis; Sarah and veteran driver Michael Regan; Brendan and Evelyn Christle; editor and writer Patrick Cunningham; Denis Bannister and Michael Carew; John Ferris and Art supremo, John de Vere White. Thanks also to Margie for putting up with the horizontal floor filing and the untidiness of two years. No doubt she will say 'And this is all you have to show for it!'

And if the format and printing of this offering delight your sensibilities, the men to see are erudite designer David Houlden, and bibliophile printer Ray Lynn of Betaprint.

# Contents

FOREWORD     11

INTRODUCTION     13

1: HORSE-DRAWN TO HORSELESS CARRIAGES     17
*Automobile's mixed reception — France and Germany lead world — repressive legislation hampers British*

2: IRELAND'S MOTORING CONTRIBUTION     23
*Dublin hosts world's first pneumatic tyre factory — inaugural Tours— Wexford's extra-terrestrial sighting — Irish drivers abroad*

3: GORDON BENNETT SPONSORS FIRST INTERNATIONAL SERIES     29
*France races ahead — flamboyant Gordon Bennett — Edge's unexpected win for Britain*

4: IRELAND CHOSEN FOR BIG RACE     37
*Round towers and Ptolemy-marked sites — Speed Trials for Dublin, Down, Cork and Kerry — 'with dust and din and a dropped gear pin!'*

5: THE PUBLIC RELATIONS OFFENSIVE     45
*Roads improved — MPs and PPs lobbied — nationalist opposition — Paris–Madrid carnage threat*

6. FINAL RACE PREPARATIONS     51
*Exemplary organisation — teams chosen — Americans' European debut — fire destroys German entries*

7: DAREDEVILS AND THE RED DEVIL — THE DRIVERS     57
*World's best represent six nations — de Knyff, hero of city-to-city marathons — Paris–Madrid victor Gabriel — record-breaker 'Red Devil' Jenatzy*

8: TEAMS, ARISTOCRACY AND FASHIONS ARRIVE     64
*Thousands welcome teams — drivers' view of course — Percy French 'Now we sing a swifter steed' — hotel overcharging — Gordon Bennett!*

9: RACE-EVE EXCITEMENT — CARS WEIGH IN     75
*Dublin 'a petrol-smelling Saturnalia' — Naas weigh-in disputes — German tyres rejected — drivers' premonitions*

10: START YOUR ENGINES!     85
*Packed trains — birds take flight —*
*'Mephistophelian' Jenatzy's fiery start — Winton stranded*

11: EVENTFUL FIRST LAP     96
*Spectators aghast at Edge's speed — Foxhall-Keene's surprise —*
*Stocks loops the loop — de Knyff survives —*
*Jenatzy and Owen confrontation*

12: JARROTT SOMERSAULTS TO DESTRUCTION     104
*Sergeant Halley's comet — Napier driver and*
*mechanic left for dead — de Caters' chivalry — Mors revels in*
*Curragh's unrestricted space*

13: FARMAN, DE KNYFF, AND JENATZY DUEL     112
*Axle failure foils Foxhall-Keene — Edge shines in adversity —*
*Gabriel plagued by misfire — Mooers jousts with hedge and mechanic*

14: BAND PLAYS ON AS STORM BATTERS DRIVERS     119
*Gabriel spins — cheers for Edge and Winton — accident rumours —*
*web-footed Jenatzy increases lead*

15: FRENCH REDUCE JENATZY'S LEAD     125
*Farman's fastest lap — de Caters' consistency — mechanics' courage —*
*de Knyff meets a jaywalker*

16: THE RED DEVIL STAMPS HIS AUTHORITY     131
*Gabriel's equine confrontation — Edge in tyre wars — Farman overtakes*
*teamleader — Winton flies into retirement*

17: JENATZY IMPRINTS FINAL TRIUMPHANT GROOVE     138
*Fastest lap underlines leader's mastery — de Knyff repasses Farman —*
*axle failure robs de Caters — Red Devil overcome by reception*

18: FROM THE COCKPIT — DRIVERS' STORIES     147
*Gabriel's frustration — Jellinek's delight — Edge disqualified —*
*Dublin welcomes 'Victorious soldiers returning' — de Knyff announces*
*retirement*

19: WORLD RECORD BROKEN IN PHOENIX PARK     155
*De Forest's 84 mph — Rolls wins in Cork and Kerry —*
*Edge's appropriate success*

20: FAREWELL TO THE TITANS     164
*Race's rich legacy — Grand Prix replaces Gordon Bennett Cup —*
*drivers' fates — Jenatzy's untimely demise*

RACE ENTRANTS, FINAL PLACINGS AND INDIVIDUAL LAP TIMES     171

REFERENCES     172

INDEX     174

# Foreword

Having won the 1950 Tourist Trophy at Dundrod and, later, a certain 1,000-mile Italian event, I have had more than a passing acquaintanceship with the thrills — and spills! — of racing on the open roads.

Hence my heightened appreciation of the great pioneering drivers. Men like Rene de Knyff, Paris–Madrid winner Fernand Gabriel and the gritty Selwyn Edge — all of whom feature in this exciting account of the 1903 Gordon Bennett Cup race, Britain's first international motor race.

No one can turn the clock back. But, occasionally, a thoughtful and faithful account can make a past event come to life. And in this *Boy's Own* chronicle of skill, drama, chivalry and inspirational sportsmanship, Brendan Lynch brings us into the heart of that distant day's epic struggle.

The drivers are three-dimensional. The thunderstorm's rain stings our faces. We flinch at the constant spray of flints from the unprotected wheels. We enjoy vivid insights into the contrasting characters of the drivers, particularly the fearless racewinner Camille Jenatzy, who later died so tragically.

This well-rounded book does justice to motor racing's pioneers and to a most exciting event, whose drama continued to the very last few miles of the day-long epic.

And, for me, there was the added personal bonus of discovering that my fifties Wakefield Trophy success at the Curragh traversed part of the circuit covered by these great drivers. Perhaps some of their spirit rode with me in that last famous road race, the Mille Miglia!

Sir Stirling Moss

The cars came scudding in towards Dublin, running evenly like pellets in the groove of the Naas Road.

> JAMES JOYCE, *After the Race*


A flashing streak of green with a comet-like tail of dust behind it appeared, flashed under the green flag, steadied for the curve, and then went roaring across the plain.

> *Irish Field*

# Introduction

In the summer evenings, full-throated birds enhance the spacious green beauty around County Kildare's tree-lined Moat of Ardscull. An amiable, overweight and calculating collie welcomes those who picnic beside the 200-year old stonewalls. Verdant and fertile, the flat countryside stretches to endless horizons. In the distance, a Millet-like spire denotes the nearest big town, Athy on the river Barrow.

It's hard to believe that a century earlier, in July 1903, this was the focus of world media attention, as the surrounding roads were raced over by some of the most revered motorsport pioneers; and acts of individual heroism and sportsmanship lifted the Gordon Bennett Cup event beyond the realms of a mere mechanical or human contest.

I used the Gordon Bennett circuit during my training nights for cycle racing. As I swung around the Moat of Ardscull under the humming telegraph lines, and the moon played tag with the windswept clouds, it didn't take much imagination to hear the ghostly approach of the huge racing cars, and the excited hubbub as spectators craned their necks to see who was roaring down the dusty road.

Was it the great bearded veteran, Rene de Knyff, his mechanic crouched low for extra streamlining — or the chivalrous Baron de Caters, the millionaire amateur who raced like a professional? Or was it the gallant 1902 winner Selwyn Edge — or the Red Devil Camille Jenatzy himself, who scattered the stones and flints as he powerslided his big Mercedes around these very bends for lap after lap of the 1903 marathon?

Later, pedalling across the vast silent Curragh, I passed clumps of frozen furze, heads low with iced winter dew. Were they sleeping or were they conversing in the quiet night? 'My great great grandfather saw Fernand Gabriel, you know! Every blossom shook as he thundered past on this very road in his big Mors. Fernand Gabriel who won the Paris–Madrid — can you imagine?'

In Ireland, where Yeats's *sidhe* and the fairies thrive, and where myth, history and reality are as firmly entwined as the Book of Kells calligraphy, the names of the Red Devil and Selwyn Edge occupy a special place in local folklore. Kildare people will happily show you where Edge's axle broke — it didn't — or where the Red Devil took off and flew over a hedge — an exaggeration. But what's so special about reality? Reality is a modern Formula One driver punting off his nearest rival in order to become World Champion. The men of the 1903 Irish Gordon Bennett Cup event were made of much more wondrous and enduring material.

The race was a pivotal event in the history of British manufacturing and Irish sport. It kickstarted the lethargic UK motor industry and bequeathed a rich and enduring legacy to the host country. Twenties cult figure Henry Segrave travelled far from his Tipperary home to break the world land speed record in 1929 and become the first person to drive at over 200 mph. Algy and Bill Guinness of the famous brewing family scored many important British and international twenties successes. Hugh Hamilton from Omagh took MG's first major win at Germany's Nurburgring in 1932. Dublin's Phoenix Park is now motor racing's oldest continuously used road circuit. Its Irish Grand Prix series and the Tourist Trophy races at the northern Ards and Dundrod venues attracted the greatest drivers who ever raced. Such legends as 'the flying Mantuan,' Tazio Nuvolari, Alberto Ascari, Juan Manuel Fangio — and scintillating Britons Stirling Moss and Mike Hawthorn, who scored their first major successes on Irish soil.

Later World Champions including Emerson Fittipaldi and Ayrton Senna raced at Kildare's Mondello Park which, together with the northern Kirkistown circuit, provided a fruitful nursery ground for Irish talent in the post-war period. Irish drivers captured a legion of British saloon and single-seater titles and international rallies. Paddy Hopkirk, Ronnie Adams and Rosemary Smith won Monte Carlo, Alpine and Tulip rallies. Ronan Morgan was one of international rallying's most successful navigators. Dublin motor-cyclists Stanley Woods and Reg Armstrong won many international Grands Prix, and Downpatrick's Joey Dunlop was the most successful ever Tourist Trophy racer. Michael Roe from Naas, down the road from the 1903 Gordon Bennett Cup course, took the 1984 US Can-Am Sportscar Championship. No fewer than nine Irish drivers progressed to Grand Prix status. John Watson and Eddie Irvine were each runners-up in the Drivers' World Championship. A nominally Irish team now competes in Formula One. No mean achievement for a small unindustrialised country on the remote fringes of western Europe — and all a result of that great race on 2 July 1903.

There is little comparison, however, between modern television-tailored Formula One and the pioneering Gordon Bennett Cup period. Unrestricted egos, greed and computerisation have replaced the idealism and human ingenuity which the great Irish event exemplified. As the *Irish Cyclist* wrote in 1903: 'One thing the Gordon Bennett race did. It showed us that the finest pluck and chivalry, and the most splendid sportsmanship, are still factors in the making of men. If motor racing did nothing but bring out such qualities as these, it is worth preserving in some shape or form.'

But as commercial interests inevitably took over, motor racing began to shed that early innocence. Irish Gordon Bennett Cup participant Charles

Jarrott saw the writing on the wall when he wrote on his retirement; 'Above all, it is now evident that racing is repeatedly being reduced to a business. The firm with the most money makes the most elaborate arrangements, and places the drivers of its cars at a corresponding advantage over its opponents.'

The centenary of Jarrott's race, however, provides a timely excuse to recall that more honourable period before avarice and computerisation eviscerated a great sport. And, particularly, the momentous day in July 1903, when motorsport's greatest drivers converged on Ireland for the first international race to be held in the British Isles. When immense crowds watched the latest technology in awe and disbelief at the power and speed of those carriages without horses. Vehicles which could do in an hour what was previously a day's journey! And drivers who could harness those machines' astonishing power and guide them around corners and up hills at a pace unmatched by the fastest racehorse. Brave and invariably unrewarded pioneers with whom Columbus and stout Cortez would have been at home.

So draw up your chair. Select a libation. Forget the rat-race. Return with wonder to the eventful early days of a new century. When the car was in its fragile untested infancy and, with death and disaster as constant companions, the high-mounted drivers who raced them on dust-enshrouded roads into an opaque and dangerous unknown were among the bravest ever seen on a race track.

*Ní bheidh a leithéidí arís ann.* Their likes will not be seen again.

A final word! The opening chapters trace the rapid evolution of the car and of motorsport. Modern speedsters may think that this delays the action. But they provide the backdrop against which the great event took place and set the race firmly in the context of the times!

*Calm before the storm. Dublin before the arrival of the automobile.*

# Map of the Course

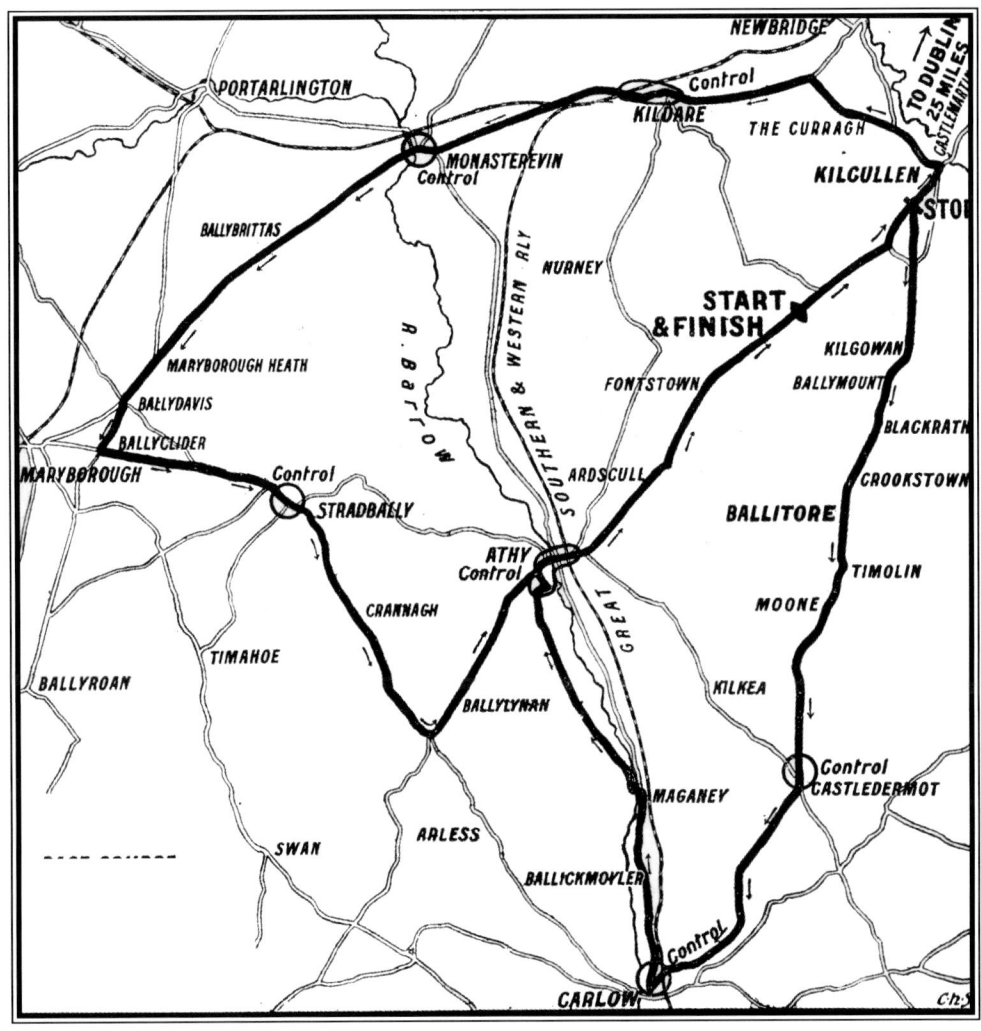

*Eastern Circuit:* Kilcullen, Timolin, Carlow, Athy, Fontstown. 40 miles.
*Western Circuit:* Kilcullen, Kildare, Maryborough, Athy, Fontstown. 51.87 miles.
*Race:* 3 laps of Eastern Circuit and 4 laps of Western Circuit. Total distance: 327.5 miles.

# 1 Horse-drawn to Horseless Carriages

Automobile's mixed reception — France and Germany lead world — repressive legislation hampers British

*Ireland, which is so long languishing in the cold shades of neglect, is today centre of a cosmopolitan interest. It is the playground for the great International game which the Twentieth Century has made its own, if it has not actually discovered. The motor is in a certain sense a symbol of the new age, and has already become developed to an extraordinary pitch of perfection. Ireland is fortunate in having been set as the scene of this great drama of speed and daring.*

Thus did Dublin's *Evening Herald* greet the bank holiday Thursday morning of 2 July, 1903, when Irish roads featured the most international endurance test of the automobile yet held. The Gordon Bennett Cup car race was the first international motorsport event to be held in the British Isles. It was marked by drama and individual acts of courage, chivalry and sportsmanship, which ensured it a rare and exalted place in the pantheon of motor-racing history. The supporting Phoenix Park Speed Trials saw the world land speed record being beaten at over 84 mph.

The event's use of a controllable lapped circuit, unlike the earlier and more hazardous city-to-city marathons, established a precedent for future competitions. Its safe running also ensured the sport's continuation, which had been in serious doubt following the previous month's Paris–Madrid race carnage. The race accelerated local acceptance of the automobile and finally kickstarted the lethargic British motor industry. It also marked an emphatic watershed between Victorian pace and ideas and the brave new world of technology.

Ireland's greatest sporting event attracted the country's largest-ever influx of foreign visitors. British MPs rubbed shoulders with Belgian barons, German counts and such French aristocrats as the banker Baron Henri de Rothschild. More importantly, the race and Speed Trials featured the first American team to compete abroad as well as no fewer than five world record-breakers and the world's top drivers representing France, Germany and Great Britain.

The list of competitors from six different countries read like a *Who's Who* of pioneer motoring. The gladiators of their era, they included the French winner of most of the early city-to-city races, the immense bearded Rene de Knyff; the Irish-American playboy and rapid amateur racer, James Foxhall-Keene; the elegant millionaire Belgian, Baron de Caters; his wild compatriot, 'Red Devil' Camille Jenatzy, first person to drive a car at 100 kph — a mile a minute; and the gallant Selwyn Edge, who had pushed his car out of an Austrian river bed to win the 1902 Paris–Innsbruck race and bring the Gordon Bennett Cup event to Great Britain and Ireland.

But while remote agricultural Ireland seemed a strange choice for a demonstration of the latest and most startling technology, the country had already established a unique place in motoring history. Dublin was the site of the world's first pneumatic tyre factory, opened in 1889 by John Boyd Dunlop and Harvey du Cros. One of the earliest motor manufacturers was Frederick York Wolseley of Carlow, who supplied some of the first British racing cars. Cork had produced Henry Ford, the man whose assembly line revolution was to make the automobile available to millions and who always insisted 'The inventor of the pneumatic tyre made the automobile possible.'

Founded in 1900 by Ballinasloe clergyman's son and former racing cyclist, R.J. Mecredy, Dublin's *Motor News* was one of Britain's most authoritative automobile journals. The leading media advocate of the new automobile was the Dublin-born tycoon, Alfred Harmsworth. His *Daily Mail* played a key role in popularising motoring and encouraging the backward British motor industry.

Having experienced a reception as equivocal as its earliest spindly chassis and tiller steering, the emerging automobile needed that support. Its arrival was enthusiastically greeted by Rudyard Kipling, who rejoiced, 'I got rid of the whole tribe of coachmen, saddlers, corn dealers, smiths and vets.' Fellow-author, A. B. Filson Young, enthused:

*Freedom on two wheels: John Boyd Dunlop founded world's first pneumatic tyre factory in Dublin.*

> *The miles, once the tyrants of the road, the oppressors of the travellers, are now humbly subject to the motor car's triumphal empire. It flattens out the world, enlarges the horizon, loosens a little the tyranny it had on time, and sets back a little the barriers of space. And man who has created and endowed it, who sits and rides upon it as upon a whirlwind, moving a lever*

here, turning a wheel there, receives in his person the revenues of the vast kingdom it has conquered.

Not all welcomed the noisy new invention, however. An *Irish Wheelman* subscriber lamented in a parody of Goldsmith; 'Ill fares the land where hastening ills a prey, Where motorists accumulate and cyclists decay!' A popular picture postcard expressed a widespread perception. It showed an automobilist greeting a gun-toting sportsman; 'Have you killed anything yet?' The sportsman replies 'No — have you?' No doubt fatigued from an excess of legal objectivity, a Limerick magistrate testily insisted: 'The autocars are the greatest curse Ireland has known since the first batch of English arrived!'

*Karl Benz (1844–1929). His mother subsidised his engineering studies by working as a laundress.*

But the fulfilment of man's dream of a self-propelled horseless carriage was as inevitable as flight. As far back as the thirteenth century, scientist Roger Bacon wrote of the day when 'we shall endow chariots with increased speed, without the aid of any animal.' By the 1890s, the bicycle had given the public a foretaste of the possibilities of individualised long-distance road transportation, and also helped to break down social barriers. Artist Ferdinand Leger welcomed the aesthetic fusion of body and machine — though a defused Auguste Renoir and his Irish writer friend, George Moore, had second thoughts after breaking their arms in falls! Thousands in England and Ireland had acquired a passion for their own speedy mechanical transport, no fewer than ten million Americans owned their own personal wheels. The world was ready for the automobile, whatever the price yet to be paid (millions of fatalities, unholy oil-wars, the pre-Nader irresponsibility of manufacturers and the merry despoilation of city and countryside alike).

*Gottlieb Daimler (1834–1900). Built petrol engine with enclosed crank-shaft and hot tube ignition.*

As automobile defenders pointed out, previous means of transport had their own attendant dangers. Two outside passengers were frozen to death in March 1812 on the Bath to Chippenham coach. Many perished in railway mishaps, while hundreds were killed each year in accidents involving horses. The equines were blamed for the spread of disease, particularly eye and intestinal infection among children. With each horse producing an estimated 45 lbs of dung daily, Londoners had to tip a crossing sweep in order to clear a path through odiferous fly-infested streets. The clatter of hooves and metal wheels frequently made conversation impossible. Automobile supporters insisted that not only would the time-saving cars be cheaper to run than horses, they would also be cleaner and safer.

The father of the petrol-engined car was a poor Karlsruhe engineer, Karl Benz. Like the best Oscar Wilde parable, his mother worked as a laundress in order to subsidise his studies after the sudden death of her husband. Benz constructed a stationery gas engine in 1880. Five years later, he made the historic marriage between a scaled-down four-stroke engine, with electric ignition and surface carburettor, and a two-seater tricycle. In 1885, compatriots Gottlieb Daimler and Wilhelm Maybach also produced a petrol engine with enclosed crankshaft and hot-tube ignition. Both Benz's three-wheeler and Daimler's first car appeared in 1886. The big advantage of petrol-engined over steam-powered cars was that they required only one kind of fuel, instead of a combination of coal and water. They were also ready to work as soon as they were started!

By 1888, Benz cars were being marketed by a Paris dealer. Daimler and Benz were the earliest commercial car producers but it was France which took an early and decisive lead in motoring and motorsport (and later in aviation). The country boasted a fine road network, ingenious engineers who had served valuable apprenticeships with steam engines, and freedom from the road legislation which restricted progress in Great Britain. France regularly produced more cars than any other country until overtaken by the U.S. in 1906.

Panhard pioneered the front-mounted engine driving the back wheels via a clutch and gearbox. Even the non-driving James Joyce waxed lyrical about the poetry of this car's motion — 'The journey laid a magical finger on the genuine pulse of life and gallantly the machinery of human nerves strove to answer the bounding courses of the swift blue animal.' Toulouse Lautrec painted the first recorded motoring portrait. As well as introducing definitive road signs, the Gauls led the way in advertising, using erotic, mythological and allegorical themes. France also gave the world such words as automobile, chauffeur, chassis, and 'horseless carriage' (*voitures sans chevaux*).

*Three Wheels: Otto Benz's first patent car, 1886.*

Britain showed less foresight. 'A new French sporting craze,' was how one London newspaper ridiculed the first 1894 Paris–Rouen reliability trial. The French Automobile Club was founded in 1895, two years before its British counterpart. De Dion Bouton's sales of 1,500 cars up to April 1901 exceeded the combined production of the three principal manufacturers in England, where strict speed limits and public hostility greatly inhibited progress. By 1902, however, when Britain imported over £1m worth of cars and components, the *Daily Express* was warning 'Car Market in Foreign Hands.'

Many of the early racing drivers such as Dunlop's London manager, Selwyn Edge, Rolls-Royce founder Charles Rolls, and the record-breaking Camille Jenatzy, graduated from cycle racing. British car manufacturers Humber, Singer, Lea-Francis, Riley and Swift likewise cut their teeth in cycle construction, as did the leading French Clement and Peugeot marques. With unexpected and advantageous results for Irish motoring, Selwyn Edge was introduced to the automobile in 1895 by French cycling champion, Fernand Charron.

The future Gordon Bennett Cup winner wrote subsequently,

*After an hour's virtually trouble-free run in Charron's two-cylinder Panhard-Levassor on the streets of Paris, I was firmly convinced that the death-knell of the horse as a means of locomotion had been sounded. There was no longer a shadow of a doubt in my mind that humanity was on brink of a metamorphosis in road transport, the like of which had only reigned in the brain of a Jules Verne. If science could produce a self-propelled vehicle, such as the one I had just tried, within a year or two of Benz and Daimler first placing a horseless carriage on the roads, what would be accomplished during the following ten years or more? Compared to what would inevitably come, Charron's car would be like Stephenson's 'Rocket' to a modern locomotive.*

The realisation of how far England lagged behind France changed the course of Edge's life:

*The possibilities were without limit, but was the Continent to be allowed to have many years start on our own country, and so gain a foothold in progress from which it would be so difficult to displace it? Deeply impressed with my first experience of a motor vehicle, I returned to England next day, with the fixed determination that I would leave no stone unturned to advance the cause of the automobile, and awaken all in this country to the possibilities of this enormous new industry which was, at that moment, in its cradle.*

In addition to *Daily Mail* support, intensive lobbying by motorists and motor manufacturers finally led to the scrapping of the British Red Flag regulation, under which a motor vehicle had to be preceded by a person with a red warning flag. The speed limit was raised from four to twelve miles per hour, and Edge and *Irish Wheelman* editor R.J. Mecredy were among those who participated in the celebratory May 1896 Emancipation Day Run from London to Brighton. Royal approval was forthcoming the following year, when the Prince of Wales, soon to be crowned King Edward V11, became a motorist. The commercial advantages of petrol-power were quickly realised by such London stores as Whiteleys. It replaced its 350 horses with motorised vans, each of which could more speedily and efficiently do the work of three horses.

By late 1903, the speed limit had been raised to 20mph. Licensing was instituted for drivers and cars, and the first Society of Motor Manufacturers and Traders' show attracted over 10,000 visitors. Prices also dropped. Exhortations 'To the Nobility and Gentry' were replaced by advertisements directed at the middle and lower orders. Increasingly more reliable and simpler to use, the car had arrived — though it took some time to be completely acceptable socially. The Hon. Evelyn Ellis received less than courtly understanding when he visited his father, Lord Howard de Walden, in his Panhard-Levassor. 'Kindly bring a little pan to catch those filthy oil drops.' he was ordered. 'Certainly, father,' he replied '— if you will bring a big pan for your carriage horses when you next visit me!'

*Four wheels: Henry Ford at the helm of his 1896 quadricycle. His assembly line revolution made the automobile available to millions.*

The burgeoning Motor Trade attracted its fair share of opportunists, few more adroit than Chicago's Edward Joel Pennington. He breezed into England where his fulsome claims to have invented an unpuncturable tyre, omnibuses, delivery vans, fire engines, and an airship airily outmatched his total output of fifteen vehicles. One of his most celebrated advertisements was for a motorised bicycle, with which he claimed to have jumped a distance of 65 feet! He managed to sell his patents for £100,000 to the British Motor Syndicate, but he was less successful in 1897 when he floated Ireland's first ever motor business. One of his few cars led a parade through the Dublin streets and the capital of £250,000 was quickly fully subscribed. But directors soon realised they had been misled and they returned subscribers' money. Pennington was last rumoured to be designing baby carriages in the American West — powered by hot air.

# Ireland's Motoring Contribution

Dublin hosts world's first pneumatic tyre factory — inaugural Tours — Wexford's extra-terrestrial sighting — Irish drivers abroad

The Ireland which awaited the 1903 Gordon Bennett Cup racers was a deprived colonial backwater. Many people were scarred by memories of the devastating Famine. It was a land of tiny farmsteads and urban tenements, suffering from decades of deprivation, political and agrarian turmoil, and a dearth of industrial development. The emigration which had decimated the country was the highest of any country in Europe. Newspapers regularly published messages from those who wished to make contact with exiled relatives. A typical 1903 appeal was that from 'Mrs Anne Mulvany of 2 Benburb Street, who wishes to hear of some of her children in America or elsewhere.'

The average wage for an unskilled worker was twelve shillings per week, and eighteen shillings for skilled. A teacher took home one pound per week. Pawnshops abounded and loans were readily available. There was affordable accompaniment for the growth industry of emigration songs, with pearl melodeons available for only 6/9d from Kearneys of Capel Street. Silver wrist watches which were guaranteed for three years cost a modest 12/6d. Cars cost between £200 and £2,500 and were only for the very rich. The lower orders saw little of the coal which the Coal and Steamship Company of Burgh Quay delivered for 17 shillings a ton.

While the Quality such as Lady Clonmel and Lady Dufferin attended the last Court Season event at Buckingham Palace, nationalists did not mourn unduly when rain washed out Dublin's final June 1903 public event, the King's birthday pageant in the Phoenix Park. They applauded J P. Nannetti MP, when he refused to give an Address 'to an English king until they will give us management of our own affairs.'

Instead, thousands of Dubliners lined the Liffey quays to see an exhibition of log rolling by London lumberjack, Tom Barton. The nine-foot 'log' was made of Bovril tins, as part of the company's advertising campaign which would include a Gordon Bennett race balloon. Another fortuitous entertainment was the search for barrels of a local brew with well-advertised beneficial qualities, which had been washed off a lighter in Dublin bay.

Sadly, two diligent searchers were ill-rewarded by a court appearance after a constable arrested them in a Dollymount cottage 'where they were having a feast of porter with some women.'

James Joyce's *Dubliners* and *Ulysses* captured both the irrepressible optimism of the Irish, and the overwhelming sense of his native city as being 'the centre of paralysis', from which the only liberation was the emigrant boat or retreat into a fantasy world. But by 1903, hope was in the air as the Wyndham Land Act went a considerable way towards regulating the Land question and ending landlordism. Artist John B. Yeats supported philanthropist Hugh Lane's efforts to establish a national art gallery. Like Florence in the Dark Ages, the paralysis was quietly nurturing a Renaissance which would blossom in the Irish Literary Revival and an increased national consciousness which would lead to Independence within twenty short years.

*John Cooney won first Irish speed competition at Navan in 1900.*

For motorists, John Boyd Dunlop's tyre was also pointing the way forward in a city where sedan chairs had been used only thirty years earlier. His invention was probably the only recorded beneficial outcome of a pain in the nether regions! After his son complained about the rough cobblestones, Dunlop made the tyre which provided both a smoother and faster ride to school. 'Bladder-wheel' and 'windbag' were some of the politer epithets directed at the revolutionary device, when it made its competition debut at Belfast's Easter 1889 Queen's College Sports. But the doubters were soon silenced. Windbag-equipped dark horse Willie Hume sensationally outraced the reigning du Cros champions of Dublin to win the three main cycling events. It was to be the first of countless Dunlop successes, the most important of which would appropriately reward Ireland with the staging of the 1903 Gordon Bennett Cup race.

Harvey du Cros Senior was a paper manufacturer of Huguenot origin. He won Irish boxing and fencing championships, and founded Bective Rangers Football Club which he captained to its first Irish title. As skilful an entrepreneur as he was a sportsman, he quickly entered into negotiations with Dunlop and the pair opened the world's first pneumatic tyre factory in Dublin's Stephen's Street later in 1889. Business flourished with the cycling boom, and the growing automobile industry soon brought the company international fame. Though the marriage of the idealistic inventor and the sharp businessman eventually foundered, Dunlop's biblical profile became one of motoring's best known trademarks. His tyres were sold all over the world. Oddly enough, he had once written to du Cros: 'I do not think my pneumatic tyre will ever be a commercial success — but I am now working on something that will be, a spring for a bicycle.'

Irishman Richard Lovell Edgeworth, father of novelist, Maria, was an outstanding road engineer. His ideas led to improved road surfacing throughout the UK and further hastened the transport revolution. On the subject of roads, the Dublin *Freeman's Journal* enthusiastically welcomed the automobile, saying it was possible that 'the motorcar, with its imperative demand for a smooth surface, may prove the chief road reformer of the near future.'

The first car to brave the Irish thoroughfares was an iron-shod Serpollet Steamer, which Belfast Professor John Shaw Brown acquired in March 1896. Weeks later, the internal combustion-engined car made its Irish debut when the enterprising Rev. Ralph Harvey hired a Benz Velo in order to raise funds for Cork Grammar School at a shilling a ride. Impressed by its smooth running, a southern paper predicted: 'Oil stops will line the road and blacksmiths will now add knowledge of paraffin to their repertory!'

Dubliner Dr. John Colohan was the first Irish person to own a petrol car, when he imported another Benz Velo later that year. He was soon joined by such prominent citizens as Lord Iveagh of the Guinness brewing family and *Freeman's Journal* editor M. H. Gillie. Restless Co-operative Movement founder, Horace Plunkett, insisted that the automobile 'furnishes an ideal combination of business and pleasure.'

Ireland's earliest contest between mechanically propelled vehicles was a motorcycle race held at the Navan sports in August 1900. It was won by the Kells cycle dealer John Cooney, a friend of nationalist leader, Charles Stewart Parnell. Impressed onlookers included future writer and motorist, Oliver St. John Gogarty, who took the supporting one-mile cycle race. Gogarty saw no conflict between the artist and the inventor, writing subsequently: 'Invention needs the same spark from heaven for the man who can bend faith by rhythm, as it does from the man who can transcend the limitations of time and space.'

The first organised Motor Tour took place in July 1900, when the Shannon Development Company arranged a trip from Dublin to Killaloe. Despite a vocabulary-enriching Curragh confrontation with a platoon of Lancers and their frightened horses, the eleven participants were welcomed all along the route. Farmers cheered from their fields and special trainloads of Limerick spectators greeted them across the river in Ballina. Variously thought to be travelling tinkers or circus men, two Daimler drivers spread the motoring gospel further by climbing Ballaghabeama Pass in Kerry, before returning home via Waterford. Lords Iveagh and Harmsworth also did their bit with separate tours.

*Oliver St. John Gogarty — 'no conflict between artist and inventor.'*

The Royal Irish Automobile Club was founded in Dublin in 1901, R.J. Mecredy and Dr. Colohan being among the few non blue-blooded members rubbing shoulders with titled landowners, decorated militarymen, brewers and distillers. Cars were still for the rich, but Henry Ford's mass-production revolution would quickly change all that. The inaugural RIAC 1,000 miles Tour of Ireland in 1901 attracted sixteen entrants, including the racer Charles Jarrott who brought five other motorists across from England. Dublin's *Freeman's Journal* greeted the automobile as 'a triumph of modern evolution — the Twelfth Centaur, combining the power of the horse magnified and the intelligence of man sharpened by the excess of voluntary peril.'

Some country folk complained that they had been given insufficient notice and were thus unable to prepare 'a proper welcome.' One lady graciously produced her best tea-cup when asked for water for a boiling radiator. Two Kilkenny schoolgirls bolted in terror from 'dem divils on wheels' when Charles Jarrott in his long black motoring macintosh and dust-glasses approached them for directions. Another automobile caused Wexford's first recorded extra-terrestrial sighting. An elderly woman who had never seen a car before was on her way to the market, when she was overtaken by pioneer motorist Colonel John Magrath. As she recovered from shock in the town, she told shoppers how she had seen 'a carriage from the other world, with a

*English racer Charles Jarrott visits Ireland. Like many of the early drivers, he had also graduated from cycle racing.*

horrible ugly demon driving it. I knew he was coming to take me to hell but I made a sign of the cross and when I looked again, thanks be to God, he had vanished in a cloud of dust!'

Irish drivers were also participating in competitions outside the country. The formidable Hercules Langrishe distinguished himself in the 1,000 Mile Tour of Great Britain in 1900, and beat Rolls-Royce founder Charles Rolls in a car trial at London's Ranelagh Gymkhana. Harvey du Cros became London's

Panhard agent and his son George acted as mechanic for Charles Jarrott when the pair finished second in the 1902 Circuit du Nord. Belfast's Leslie Porter and Willie Nixon entered for the last of the great city-to-city events, the ill-fated Paris–Madrid race. Jerry O'Connor's Macy-sponsored Benz dominated the first-ever U.S. event at Chicago in 1895 until, just miles from the flag, the impetuous Irishman crashed — for the third time! Henry Ford won the 1901 Grosse Point race (in 1904, he became the only manufacturer ever to break the world speed record in a petrol car of his own construction). Waterford's Joe Tracy was one of America's most successful early drivers. He would later become the only Irishman to contest the Gordon Bennett Cup, the world's first international motor racing series.

*Belfast's Leslie Porter and Willie Nixon entered ill-fated Paris–Madrid race.*

# Gordon Bennett Sponsors First International Series

France races ahead — flamboyant Gordon Bennett — Edge's unexpected win for Britain

The Gordon Bennett Cup series commenced in 1900 in France, which had staged all the early major motor races. 'Win on Sunday, sell on Monday,' was the motto of its enterprising manufacturers. They had found that competition led to greater efficiency and reliability for their Bollee, Clement, Darracq, De Dion Bouton, Mors, Panhard, Peugeot and Renault machines.

These constructors dominated the early motoring world. Their advances in power transmission and design were imitated wherever new firms sprang up. Some fearless French pioneers had an almost Messianic belief in the necessity of racing. The Marquis de Dion said 'Each time, I considered the danger and the possibility of an accident, I accepted the possible consequences. My fellow-drivers thought as I did. The future of the automobile is more important than our lives. Nothing can interfere with progress.'

French physicians were the first to find that high speeds apparently intoxicated some drivers! A magazine explained:

> *Normally, the lungs contain air of three conditions; freshly inspired air, charged with oxygen; air ready to be expired, charged with carbonic acid gas and other impurities; and the so-called residual air, stored in the furthest spaces of the lungs, which is giving its oxygen to the blood and is removing from the blood carbonic acid and other waste products.*
>
> *Ordinarily, the exchange is slow and gradual, but in motoring, not only is the breath quickened and the flow-tide of fresh air and oxygen therefore hastened, but moreover, the fresh oxygen-charged air blows actively into the lungs and quickens and freshens the residual air store. Now, oxygen is a strong stimulant to the brain and the nervous system. Hence the mental exhilaration which results from motoring and the long deep draughts of fresh air taken in. Motorists indeed require no other stimulant and men accustomed to feeling the need for occasional alcoholic 'fillip' lose their interest, and find it much diminished while motoring.*

A conclusion which must have sounded alarm bells among more sociable automobilists! But early speedsters endured an uncomfortable trip to their oxygen-charged Nirvana. The first racing cars were crude and brutish affairs. Almost springless, their immense slow-turning engines shook both the ground and the wooden chassis, and sent shock waves up the flimsy steering columns. Handling and braking capabilities lagged way behind their immense power. Controlling these high-geared leviathans required a rare combination of Herculean strength and finesse with speed control. There was no throttle regulator as in later cars, engines ran at a constant speed, with sliding change-speed gears.

Perched high over narrow-tyred wooden wheels which were a yard in diameter, the drivers were fearless pioneers who charted unexplored territory. Each turn of the wheel led into an exciting but hazardous unknown. They coughed and cursed and held oil-stained scarves over their faces, as they attempted to pass their rivals. The romance of the roads mantled a harsh reality. Many paid with their lives, like Emile Levassor, winner of the first motor race and also the sport's first casualty.

That opening event was staged in 1895 over a daunting 732 miles from Paris to Bordeaux and back. Ignoring the derisive catcalls of horsemen who occasionally sprinted past him, Levassor drove his solid rubber-tyred 3½ hp Panhard single-handed for 48 hours to win at an average speed of 15 mph. Edouard Michelin gave the pneumatic tyre its race debut in that event. He finished last after 22 punctures. But within two years almost all cars were fitted with pneumatic tyres.

The earliest event to cross an international frontier was the 1898 Paris–Amsterdam–Paris race which was won by Fernand Charron. His Panhard averaged 27 mph for the 890 miles, an indication of the fledgling automobile's rapid progress. The courage of the racing pioneers was matched by their resourcefulness. When Charron was stricken by transmission trouble in the Tour de France, he drove in reverse for 25 miles before finally accepting defeat!

Perhaps the most bizarre race of all was the 1899 104-mile Paris–Trouville competition for runners, cyclists, motorcyclists, horses and cars. With a 14-hour headstart (the runners had 20 hours, cyclists five and motorcyclists three and a quarter hours), two horses scored a majestic 8.5 mph swansong success. A motorcyclist averaged 32.5 mph to finish ahead of the first 35.2 mph car. It was to be the last recorded victory of one horse over multiple horsepower.

As Gordon Bennett shrewdly observed, motor racing proved an irresistable draw and the starts of the early events attracted unprecedented crowds. British driver Selwyn Edge recalled the chaos of the 1899 Paris–Bordeaux race:

*Perched high over narrow-tyred wooden wheels — pioneer racer Rene de Knyff.*

*Pandemonium broke out; the engines of the unsilenced cars roared, motor tricyclists pedalled for dear life, cars ran on to the footpath, pedestrians and cyclists hurled themselves into places of safety. Several engines refused to fire, while others gave forth a half-hearted explosion or two and then stopped. Minor collisions were frequent.*

For some participants the racing was purely a sport. The flying landscape, the tantalising endless road, the wind in one's face and the mighty sound of the engines — some as large as twelve litres! — all provided superlative thrills. For those who couldn't afford an automobile, it was the height of drama to watch and identify the racers, any one of whom might be killed, as they flashed past in a blue haze of burning oil. The giant cars raised immense clouds of dust. An observer wrote: 'As a speeding monster raced by, with stones, sticks and leaves flying in its vortex, a great cloud of dust rose up instantly cloaking the car from view, and only the dust cloud, the beat of the engine, and the maddened snort of the exhaust dying away in the distance told that anything had passed.'

*Flamboyant James Gordon Bennett sponsored first international race series.*

The contests also proved an incomparable advertising medium for the manufacturers. They had news value. The media covered every race and reliability trial, a win guaranteeing priceless publicity. Clubs were formed in many towns and cities, which in turn organised regional events. The gospel of the automobile spread, and the pace and growing reliability of the cars impressed even the most sceptical. As speeds increased, the races from Paris to Bordeaux, Rouen, Berlin, and Vienna dramatically shrunk distances from the hub of the French capital, and hastened a transport and social revolution that no one could have previously forecast.

Anglo-Irish driver Moore-Brabazon of Tara, who was to compete in the Gordon Bennett Irish Fortnight, wrote:

> *The crucible of competition quickly eliminated the weak and badly prepared machines and soon produced an increasingly effective all-purpose vehicle. It inevitably led to better roadholding, more effective suspension, improved electrical systems, brakes and carburation, greater all-round reliability, and increased comfort and safety for drivers and passengers of ordinary cars. The weight limit for the Gordon Bennett cars, for example, also had a remarkable effect on design, keeping everything light and encouraging the study of metallurgy in order to get power without weight.*

For better or worse, speed soon became the keynote of the new twentieth century. In shipping, trains and telegraphy, it marked an end to Victorian tempo and ushered in an age of scientific progress in which the internal-combustion engine played a major role. French racer Henri Fournier reiterated to 21-year old James Joyce in manifesto-like terms: 'Motoring will prove to be the greatest benefactor of mankind, and will materially alter the conditions and outlook of life. The greatest future lies before mechanical invention. Wait only until people have become reconciled to it and its splendid possibilities. Such events as the Paris–Madrid and the Gordon Bennett Cup will materially help towards this end.'

The arrival of an international motoring competition was inevitable. Prior to national Grand Prix events, the Gordon Bennett Cup races provided a rare opportunity for different countries to compare and promote their cars.

*James Joyce interviewed leading French driver, Henri Fournier.*

Race series founder James Gordon Bennett was the first of motorsport's many flamboyant sponsors. He was born in New York in May 1841 to immigrant Meath music teacher, Henrietta Agnes Crean, and Scottish-born newspaper owner James Gordon Bennett. With money on tap, his early life was devoted to sport and gambling. His social charm was matched by his eccentricities. He once rode a coach and four from Rhode Island to Central Park stark naked, for a wager. In 1886, he initiated the first transatlantic yacht race when he successfully raced a New York rival from Sandy Hook, New Jersey, to the Isle of Wight for a $90,000 wager. Four years later, he made his only Irish visit when he completed a return race from Cobh to Sandy Hook.

That marked his only visit to Ireland. Capricious and autocratic, one contemporary one described him as 'the beau devil of the man of the world and all-around daredevil.' Another said that when sober the American displayed the worst qualities of the Scotch and, when drunk, the worst qualities of the Irish! But he also had a charitable side. He sponsored a soup kitchen in the New York slums and in 1882 he established a fund 'for the relief of distress in Ireland.'

Tall and handsome, with sharp blue eyes and a bristling moustache, 'Jimmy' — as he was known to his few close friends — was much in demand by the ladies. But his engagement to prominent Baltimore socialite, Caroline May, came to an abrupt and un-parlourlike end. He arrived drunk to her New Year's Day 1877 party and relieved himself in the grand piano. Caroline's brother then challenged Bennett to a duel. Fortunately for the future of Irish and international motor racing, both parties missed. Bennett's family was no doubt even more relieved when he agreed to represent the *New York Herald Tribune* in Paris.

But New York's loss was Europe's gain. Gordon Bennett had inherited a keen sense of the newsworthy and he soon proved to be a media innovator. He introduced biotype and daily weather forecasts to Europe, as well as wireless telegraphy for sending news dispatches. The American was typical of the colourful newspaper proprietors of the turn of the century. He enjoyed a lavish lifestyle aboard his Mediterranean-moored yacht *Lysistrata* — whose complement included two Jersey cows to provide milk 'free of germs and adulteration!'

But unlike William Randolph Hearst or Alfred Harmsworth of the *Daily Mail* empire, he did not put his money into fast cars, art or Gothic follies. Instead, he publicised his *Tribune* with a series of spectacular publicity stunts such as Artic and African expedition sponsorships. He was responsible for Henry Morton Stanley's 1869 search for explorer David Livingstone. This resulted in the most famous journalistic scoop of all time and the universally quoted greeting — 'Mr. Livingstone, I presume!'

The newspaper magnate was a founding member of both the Automobile Club de France and of the committee which guaranteed funds for the inaugural 1895 Paris–Bordeaux race. But he never drove a car or attended any of the events he sponsored! He realised the publicity potential of motor racing after attending the Boulevard Maillot start of the historic 1894 Paris–Rouen Trial. It was at his *New York Herald* office that Fernand Charron deposited 20,000 francs as a sign of his acceptance of a 1,000-mile endurance challenge by the American, Alexander Winton. Nothing came of the 1899 challenge, but a month later the newspaper magnate offered the famous international trophy.

While the Gordon Bennett Cup immortalised his name, the trophy was officially named the *Coupe Internationale*. It was always referred to as such in Bennett's newspaper and by the man himself who, ironically, eschewed personal publicity. His intention was to encourage international rivalry and to provide a means of ascertaining automobile progress; 'In the absence of periodic trials, makers of one nationality would be able to live on their reputation, while others might be turning out as good or better vehicles. With the institution of a challenge cup, manufacturers would have to fight to uphold their reputation, while those who claimed to build cars equally as good, would find an excellent opportunity of substantiating their claims.'

An outstanding period piece, the solid silver trophy was executed in Paris by the fashionable Rue de la Paix silversmith, Andre Aucoc. It weighed seventeen kilograms and cost 12,000 francs. Mounted on a mottled marble plinth, the trophy mirrored the grace and movement of the *Quadriga* chariot of Peace at London's Hyde Park Corner. Guided by the Spirit of Progress carrying a torch, it depicted the lightly clad and delicately balanced winged goddess of Victory braving the sculptured wind in the laurel-leaved driver's seat of a racing Panhard.

The Gordon Bennett International Trophy was to be contested by teams of three cars, each nominated by a recognised national club. Every part of the car had to be made in the country of origin, drivers and entrants representing national clubs were to be members of those clubs. Three cars meant that a small nation had parity with a larger manufacturing one. National colours were also suggested, though these were not rigidly enforced until the 1903 Irish race. The colours were white for Germany, red for America, yellow for Belgium, blue for France and green for Great Britain (since the allegedly lucky colour was used by Jarrott in the 1901 Paris–Berlin race to offset his unlucky 13 race number). Cars should be two-seaters, with both seats occupied all the time. Drivers and mechanics were to weigh no less than 70 kg. apiece — any shortfall had to be made up with ballast! The weight of the car when empty was to be not less than 400 kilograms and not over 1,000 kilograms.

Race organisation costs were to be divided between the clubs and race distance was to be between 550 and 650 kilometres. It was at first proposed that results should be judged by points, the placings of the vehicles being reckoned and the Cup going to the team with the smallest number of points. But it was finally decided that the prize would have more impact by being awarded to the winning vehicle. The race was to be run annually between 15 May and 15 August by the country holding the Cup. France was to stage the inaugural competition on June 14, 1900.

Acrimony clouded that first Paris–Lyon event. The French team was an all-Panhard choice, despite the recent successes of the rival Mors car. Many local authorities at first refused permission for the race. The organisation was so casual that Belgium's Camille Jenatzy, and many other drivers lost their way. Sheep and straying animals caused further havoc. Fernand Charron lost control at 60 mph, when a St. Bernard dog wedged itself between the right wheel and spring and jammed the steering. But the former cycling champion regained the road and overcame a damaged axle to win from his compatriot, Leonce Giradot. Charron's time for the 353 miles was nine hours and nine minutes, an average of 38.6 mph. Alexander Winton, whose challenge to Charron had indirectly led to the series, retired after buckling a front wheel. An observer commented: 'America has most things to learn in the craft of building a motor car.'

*Irish Gordon Bennett competitor Camille Jenatzy, first to drive at a mile a minute in this car in 1899.*

The following year's race was run in conjunction with the Paris–Bordeaux event. The Germans were unable to prepare a team in time and Selwyn Edge was forced to abandon due to unsuitable tyres. Giradot won at an average of 37 mph, after valve trouble had eliminated Charron. The Gordon Bennett Cup's international function was diluted in 1902 when Mercedes declined to compete, despite the enthusiasm of its most energetic dealer, Emil Jellinek. The 351-mile race took place over the toughest route yet from Paris to Innsbruck. The only challenge to the all-conquering French came from Selwyn Edge's Napier and Claude Grahame-White's Wolseley. Race favourite Henri Fournier abandoned with clutch trouble, leaving Rene de Knyff well ahead of the Napier. But the French veteran broke down just after the summit of the 5,000-foot Arlberg Pass. A broken pump stranded Edge's punctured Napier before the sporting Count Eliot Zborowski stopped to help. Despite having virtually no brakes, Edge went on to snatch a sensational and historic 31.8 mph victory in his Dunlop-shod car.

The Napier driver's win marked the first international motor racing success by an English car. It was also a rare triumph of mind over matter. Edge had not slept for two nights prior to the start, having twice had to rebuild the untested Napier's gearbox — once on the Boulogne ferry. Unaccustomed to losing, French officials sought to have the racewinner disqualified for allegedly receiving outside assistance after his car had fallen into a riverbed. Rene de Knyff sportingly intervened and nothing more was heard of the protest. Edge's win gained valuable prestige for British manufacturers whose exports tripled by the end of 1902. It stimulated local automobile interest and finally introduced motorsport to the British Isles.

More importantly, Edge's success was fortuitous for the future of the Gordon Bennett series. Had a French car won, the 1903 Cup event would not have been held as racing was banned in France following the Paris–Madrid debacle that May. Napier's defeat of the hitherto unassailable French additionally encouraged other manufacturing countries and achieved Gordon Bennett's vision of genuine international competition. The 1903 race would be no mere Anglo-French duel, but a four-country contest which would also include Germany and the USA.

Selwyn Edge was treated to a celebratory banquet in London, where French driver Leonce Giradot formally handed over the Gordon Bennett Cup. Britain's opportunity to stage the race, defend the Cup and revitalise its backward auto business seemed likely, however, to be swamped by insurmountable odds. The English had developed canals and railways at the expense of their roads, which featured none of the long stretches available on the continent. There were proposals to utilise the flat empty roads of Lincolnshire and Scotland and to build a track at picturesque Purley, south of London, an idea which received an emphatic '*Non*' from the French. With a rigidly enforced speed limit, no race track and public hostility against the automobile, where could the event be held?

*Selwyn Edge's sensational 1902 Gordon Bennett Cup success led to Ireland hosting the big 1903 race.*

# 4 Ireland Chosen for Big Race

Round towers and Ptolemy-marked sites — Speed Trials for Dublin, Down, Cork and Kerry — 'with dust and din and a dropped gear pin!'

By 1903 people were adjusting to the new century. Though change was in the air, the international news still had a familiar ring. Hundreds of Jews were massacred in a Russian pogrom at Kishinev, while 20 workers were killed in an explosion at London's Woolwich Arsenal. Pope Leo XIII was fighting for his life in Rome. Paul Gauguin died in the Marquesas at the age of 54, *Call of the Wild* was establishing the reputation of the turbulent Jack London.

On the technological front, the first outdoor telephone kiosk opened in London. The Wright brothers filed a patent for a plane based on the glider that they had successfully flown six months earlier. Recovering from February's disastrous Big Wind, Irish people welcomed the news that Henry Ford was preparing to sell his first production line Model A car. Intrepid Waterford explorer H. H. Deasy followed up his Nice Touring Car gold medal by becoming the first to drive a car up the mountain from Montreaux to Riches des Naye. But these events were overshadowed by growing rumours that the country might be selected to host the great international motor race for the Gordon Bennett Cup.

The secretary of the Automobile Club of Great Britain and Ireland (the ACGBI), Claude Johnson, was the first to suggest Ireland as a suitable venue. As the bandwagon of interest began to roll, others were quick to also claim credit. Like *Motoring Illustrated*, the *Irish Field* reiterated that 'some time ago, we drew attention to Ireland as a venue for motor racing.' With readily available resources, particularly stone and cheap labour, the establishment of the Board of Works in 1830 and the later Famine Relief building programmes ensured that the country boasted an extensive network of solid and well-maintained roads. By 1861, Carlo Bianconi's yellow and crimson coaches were daily illuminating over 4,000 miles of highway from Cork to Donegal.

On 22 July, 1902, Claude Johnson asked Richard Mecredy if he could suggest a suitable course, possibly a 50 miles circuit. which could be lapped seven times to make a race distance of 350 miles. The *Motor News* proprietor — who had known Selwyn Edge from their cycle racing days — responded enthusiastically. In November, there was a rare unity of Saxon energy and Celtic ardour as English and Irish officials inspected nominated areas to the south and west of Dublin.

One of the most partisan supporters of an Irish course was the Polish-born racer, Count Eliot Zborowski. The Count had earlier lived in Ireland and hunted with the Wards, the Kildares and other leading packs, and led in winning chasers at Fairyhouse and Punchestown courses. A fastidious dresser who invariably discarded his dustcoat at race controls to reveal himself in spotless attire, Zborowski was described by Selwyn Edge as the 'Prince of good sportsmen.' He had refused to protest when French chicanery deprived him of a well-deserved success in the recent Paris to Vienna motor race.

On their second winter trip to Ireland, Zborowski, Selwyn Edge and Irish pioneers Bill Peare and Sir William Goff examined potential circuits in the Dublin area. Zborowski compared the northern suburbs of Finglas and Mulhuddert to the Circuit des Ardennes course, but he felt that the French would object to a circuit there as being too short. The group studied a route from Tallaght suburb to Dunlavin and Timolin, but concluded that its winding roads were unsuitable for racing cars. They eventually favoured a circuit based south of Naas, which was well served by road and railways and was close to Dublin. Originally, a double circular route was considered incorporating Naas and Abbeyleix, while another idea was to link the Galway road with Naas and Maryboro (now called Portlaoise), but there was no suitable connection from Kilbeggan through Tullamore.

*Richard Mecredy helps to choose a course.*

Shortly after reserving race accommodation with the de Burgh family at Oldtown, Count Zborowski found that news of the automobile's potential had preceded him. In reply to his query about the distance to Kilcullen, a labourer replied 'It's ten miles, sir — but in one of dem yokes, it ought to be much less!' (A welcome foreshortening of the usual 'mile and a bit' reply in which the bit was invariably a mile multiplied!) But while children marvelled at the rainbow patterns left in water-filled potholes by the ungainly oily machines, others were less convinced of their efficacy. The group met a decidedly under-impressed Kildare man, who insisted 'I don't think I'd care to go through the world so quick. My old donkey will carry me quickly enough into the next world, and what's the use in hurrying when you can't come back?'

While the circuit was being considered, there was also the small problem of obtaining legal sanction for the race. This didn't unduly worry one Irish columnist who wrote 'The English are far too law-abiding altogether, we are prepared to hold the race, official approval or not!' As a speed limit of 12 mph was strictly enforced throughout the United Kingdom, an Act of Parliament was required before the Gordon Bennett Cup event could be staged on Irish roads. The Honorable John Scott Montagu drafted the Light

Locomotives (Ireland) Act 1903, which exempted cars from any statutory speed limits on the day of the race (this precedent paved the way for such future road events as the Isle of Man Tourist Trophy motorcycle races). The Bill also absolved local councils from all road improvement expenses, a gift horse which no sensible council could decline. Claude Johnson canvassed MPs and received 57 positive replies, though not all could write back directly. The son of nationalist MP John Redmond apologised that 'Mr. Redmond is currently in prison under the Coercion Act!'

Supporters of the legislation included such fiercely divided Irish MPs as Redmond, Tim Healy, and Sir Edward Carson. As the *Northern Whig* commented 'We see a wonderful blending of the Orange and Green. There is about this matter a unanimity of which some people considered Irishmen to be incapable.' High-revving MP Cathcart Watson did not share that consensus. He complained 'A few people claim the right to drive the public off the road. Harmless men, women, and children, dogs and cattle have all got to fly for their lives at the bidding of these slaughtering, stinking engines of iniquity.'

*Racer Count Eliot Zborowski lobbied hard for Irish venue.*

His concern proved unavailing. The Bill was passed in record time and received the Royal Assent on 27 March, 1903, only seven days after its first reading. The road was now clear for the great race to be held in Ireland. Ambitious plans were also announced for an Irish Fortnight which would include one of the biggest international Speed Trials ever held. This was scheduled for Dublin's Phoenix Park and would be followed by further Speed Trials at Cork, hill climbs from Kerry in the south to northern Castlewellan, an automobile exhibition at Dublin's Earlsfort Terrace ice rink, and the world's first powerboat race in Cork. Ireland was in for a unique feast of speed.

Midlands Councils such as Kildare, Kilkenny, Queen's County and Westmeath passed flowery resolutions of welcome for the race and accompanying visitors. These were matched by equally enthusiastic media approval. *The Irish Times* was first off the line. It reiterated:

*The race is now one of the chief topics of conversation in Dublin. There is not a dissentient voice. Everybody is anxious to see the modern marvels perform their wonderful feats of speed under the control of the champion motorists of the world. It is not too much to say that Ireland is hungry for the race, and that Mr. Wyndham would perform a very popular act if he announced his intention of taking care that she will not be deprived of her desire. This race, once held, would only be the beginning, we must reasonably hope, of a series of equally interesting, exciting and profitable contests.*

While a Scottish newspaper deplored the event with national frugality ('It necessitates a great waste of petrol'), the *Pall Mall Gazette*, with some reservations, pointed out another advantage for Ireland:

*We are no friends of motor racing. As a sport, it seems to us to be too dangerous to be ever widely adopted; while it has no effect on the real motor-car industry, as the car for racing and the car for driving are as far asunder as the Poles. There is one good feature about the race, and that is that our sister island is getting such a grand crowd of tourists, as rarely falls to her lot, save on occasions of a Royal visit. Whoever loses the race, Ireland will, at any rate, be the winner!*

The Irish passion for sport and an indefinable but stirring empathy with the free-wheeling spirit of the revolutionary means of transport guaranteed a lively interest in the race. One of the warmest welcomes for the country's quantum leap into a brave new technological world was voiced by the *Northern Whig*. The Belfast paper insisted 'The race is the most important event in the history of sport in Ireland. For the time being, there is not one of the products of modern skill which more emphatically differentiates the new world from the old, than the motorcar.'

In March 1903, the Gordon Bennett Cup committee finally selected an Athy-based circuit to host the big July 2 race. Its most northerly point was only 27 miles from Dublin, and the best vantage areas were easily accessible by road. There were fast direct links by rail from the capital to such circuit towns as Kildare, Newbridge, Monasterevin, Maryboro and Athy.

The race would commence between Athy and Kilcullen, half a mile south west of Ballyshannon Cross-roads in the townsland of Tippeenan. Competitors would race north to Kilcullen, then southwards through Timolin, Moone and Castledermot to Carlow. They would return along the Barrow river bank to Athy, before recrossing the start and finish line to complete the shorter 40-mile eastern loop. Reaching Kilcullen for a second time, they would head west across the great horse-racing plain of the Curragh to Kildare, Monasterevin and the Heath of Maryboro. Then, it was left for the climb to Stradbally and Windy Gap, before returning northwards to Athy and the finish line. This section measured 51.87 miles. The race would consist of three laps of the shorter circuit and four of the longer western route, a total distance of 327.5 miles.

Though lacking the arduous climbs of the 1902 event, the course provided a much more demanding test of both man and machine than the straighter continental roads. It combined a series of long straights and twisty sections with acute and sweeping bends. There was a variety of uphill and downhill gradients — and a sufficiency of capricious bumps and humps to test the strongest springs and axles. 'The circuit is ideal for racing,' Charles Jarrott reiterated. 'But I am afraid we will be too busy competing to reflect on the exciting history or admire the splendid views!'

The circuit traversed leafy roads and hill and river vistas which would have enraptured Constable and Wordsworth. It featured a Claude Lorraine treasure trove of ancient regal and monastic sites, and areas famous from the time of Ptolemy to that of the nineteenth century statesman, Edmund Burke. The Rock of Dunamase — Fort of the Plains — recorded by the great Alexandrian, had provided a strategic and secure base for Irish chieftains until the last of the Moore clan were driven out by that ardent republican, Oliver Cromwell. But not even Cromwell's explosives were sufficient to demolish their stronghold, whose walls and massive masonry still defiantly crowned the distinctive midlands landmark. Nearby was another reminder of the frailty of dynasties, a neglected church with the graves of strangely-named and forgotten settlers.

*Typical road surface on Stradbally exit for Windy Gap.*

Near the Naas home of the kings of Leinster, Kilcullen on the river Liffey boasted the ruins of a famous ninth-century monastery. A *New Ireland Review* writer recollected its monks 'who patiently went on their quiet deliberate journeys on foot, staff in hand and wallet at their side, and who would have considered this headlong mode of transition as the most unholy exertion, destined to bring its own retribution.'

Castledermot had been home to the King of Ulidia's son, Disert-Diarmuid, who had founded another monastery there in 800 AD. As well as a distinctive round tower and Romanesque ruins, the town also boasted a fine castle built in 1180. Home of Impressionist artist Frank O'Meara, Carlow was distinguished by the ivy-covered remains of a thirteenth-century Norman castle and a dolmen whose 100-ton capstone was the largest in Ireland. Athy's graceful Barrow bridge was guarded by the sixteenth century White's Castle, while the nearby 55-foot-high Norman-built Moat of Ardcsull was famous for its commanding Midlands views.

The quiet town of Kildare with its round tower had been the fifth century base of Ireland's favourite female Christian, St. Brigid. According to an old poem, the adventurous Brigid enjoyed fast trips across the Curragh in a chariot drawn by two horses. A 1903 scribe felt that, unlike the Naas monks, the realistic saint would have welcomed the Gordon Bennett speedsters.

*We can picture her from her lonely cell under 'the goodly faire oak' likening the passage through life of some storm-tossed soul to the passing of those panting, hurrying visions — never at peace, but suggesting ambition, exertion and competition in every line of their build. But her practical mind would have rejoiced at the triumph of human ingenuity in thus making time and space subservient to the needs and enrichment of human nature.*

*A chariot fit for St. Brigid, the Coupe Gordon Bennett.*

The Curragh's massive 3,500 hectare limestone plain was best known for the breeding and training of some of the world's best racehorses and Derby, Grand National and Classics winners galore. But the Curragh had resounded to French accents long before the thunder of Fernand Gabriel's Gordon Bennett Cup Mors shook the furze bushes. Five thousand French soldiers were among the 10,000 troops based there prior to the Battle of the Boyne in 1690. And, a century later, no fewer than 13,000 British soldiers stood ready to repel a possible French invasion and those frightfully subversive concepts of *liberté, égalité* and *fraternité*.

Nearby Maryboro was named after Queen Mary, who had visited Ireland in the sixteenth century with her husband, King Philip of Spain. Ballitore was the home of the explorer, Ernest Shackleton, whose family's school provided an early education for the political philosopher and orator, Edmund Burke.

The Barrow river valley was an important centre for narrative high crosses in Ireland. One of the most inspirational sites on the race circuit was the leafy setting of the High Cross of Moone, beside the quiet Griese river. Its patiently carved relief panels were the television of the time. They relayed Christian parables to the marvelling forbears of those who were now about to witness another technological milestone.

As well as the ruins of Rheban Castle, a variety of gracious country houses and Georgian mansions also dotted the landscape. The contrast between the old and modern was piquantly noted by a journalist who observed the international automobile invasion of stone lion-sentried Ballyshannon House.

*It is a curious sight to see this romantic picturesque place, redolent of bygone hospitalities and quiet family life, now invested with stirring movement and activity. What agitated confabulations must the two old lions hold on moonlight summer nights, when those untiring spirits — the members of the club — have finished and retired to rest? What shaking of heads must they indulge in at the sight of the pantings and puffings, and the furious zeal of the Daimlers, the Wintons, the Panhards and De Dions, the monsters which have taken the place of the barouches and the coupes, so long familiar to the guardians of the peace of Ballyshannon House?*

*Instead of Big Brian, the footman, with his 'Where to, my lady?' and the stepping out of the bays to pay that visit twelve miles off, quite a day's journey, we have Monsieur le Chauffeur. Instead of 'her ladyship' in crinoline and puce silk, we have Miss Columbia van Wanderer (New York) in reindeer motorcoat and glasses. Instead of a day's jaunt, we have 'Goodbye for the present, just off to Athy, back in an hour!*

*'Ah!' sigh the lions, 'autre temps, autre moeurs!'*

Not everyone showed reverence for cherished Irish history. London's *Motoring Illustrated* was castigated for its facetious course description, when it wrote 'On the left side of the last straight stretch, the motorists will pass a very ancient burial ground, supposed to be so full of Irish Kings that there is no more room — even for a small prince. It is now surrounded by a stone wall that keeps the cattle and pigs from browsing upon such regally nourished grass.'

Mountmellick District Council passed a resolution deploring what they perceived as the offensive nature of the article. Richard Mecredy's green corpuscles also reached their rev limit. He testily observed 'The English never seem to appreciate the Irish sentiments and reverence for the memory of the great men who made this country 'the Isle of Saints and scholars' when England was completely uncivilised.' Luckily Mecredy was absent when fellow *Motor News* proprietor James C. Percy requested the French driver, Fernand Gabriel, to refrain from blowing his horn when passing the same graveyard — 'in case the dead should think it was the angel Gabriel's last trumpet and rise prematurely!' *Motoring Illustrated*'s editor subsequently apologised for the article, which had been written in his absence by a new reporter.

Athy was to be one of the busiest towns on race day, being common to both the eastern and western circuits. As interest in the Gordon Bennett grew, it wasn't long before locals were singing a new version of their most popular song;

*While going the road to sweet Athy,*
*Hurroo! Hurroo!*
*Through Carlow village to Sweet Athy,*
*Chuff-chuff! Hurroo!*
*Through Old Kilcullen to Sweet Athy*
*Wid wan black goggle in either eye,*
*I heard an Oirish Damsl cry*
*Och, Chuffy, Oi hardly knew ye.*
*With dust and din, and a dropped gear-pin,*
*The enemy nearly slew ye!*
*My darling, dear, you're out av gear!*
*Och, Chuffy, Oi hardly knew ye.*

'Going the road to sweet Athy' via tricky corner at Old Kilcullen.

# 5  The Public Relations Offensive

Roads improved — MPs and PPs lobbied — nationalist opposition — Paris–Madrid carnage threat

The pace of circuit preparations rivalled that of the competing racers. On 18 April, county surveyors, race officials and leading drivers Charles Jarrott, Charles Rolls and Selwyn Edge held a final meeting to confirm the course, mark the controls and detail the necessary improvements.

'That's a fine wall,' Edge wryly observed, as he surveyed the stout obstruction which awaited those who failed to negotiate the sharp and adverse-cambered right-angled corner at Kilcullen. The English driver's experience proved invaluable in advising circuit modifications. When he suggested cutting back the edges where the Curragh joined the Kildare road, a council official suggested that drivers would know the route by the change of direction in the line of spectators. 'They will notice nothing but the road one foot ahead of them,' the 1902 winner advised the office troglodyte.

*Checking out the course — de Dion and de donkey!*

Many corners had to be smoothed out, culverts filled in and narrow areas widened. Though the Big Wind had felled dangerous trees, several more had to be pruned, and hedges trimmed for better visibility. Resurfacing was required for some stretches including the run from Ballylinan to Athy and the final four miles between Castledermot and Carlow. In addition to the government support, the ACGBI also launched a fund to subsidise the improvements —

with the additional incentive of a £5. 2s prize for the contractor whose work was adjudged the best. In order to reduce any possible dust hazard, the start area and approaches to all dangerous corners were to be treated with Westrumite. A German concoction, this dust-retardant consisted of tallow and turpentine mixed with water.

Anglo-Irish approval for the course was not matched by French sentiments. The *Petit Parisien* haughtily insisted 'Compared to our roads, the circuit is a bad country lane.' Miffed that the race did not return to France, as had been hoped, fellow-scribes agreed that the roads were inferior to those of the most outlying French districts, and that negotiating the corners 'would be like an equestrian act in a circus.' *Matin* complained about the dangers of the sites earmarked for stands. All this, despite approval for the complete arrangements by no less a figure than the eminent racer, Rene de Knyff! And the praise of fellow entrant, Percy Owen who countered 'We couldn't have better roads. They are marvellous, nothing in America can compare, and they are as good as any in France, though not so wide.' The sensationalist French reportage was a new phenomenon for the Irish. Dublin's *Evening Mail* calmly countered 'We are not aware that they do things better in France — witness the Paris–Madrid motor race disaster.'

*Rolls-Royce founder Charles Rolls inspected the course.*

In addition to lobbying 120 MPs and 90 peers, the ACGBI also circularised 30 County Councils, 26 mayors, 41 railway companies, 450 hotels and 300 newspapers. The thrust of the club's letter was both race safety and the benefits to the Irish economy. Wisely aware of majority Catholic sentiment, the club wrote to 13 Parish Priests and the Bishop of Kildare and Leighlin. They pointed out that the event was planned for the public holiday of 2 July so as not to infringe Sabbath sensibilities. The Bishop immediately declared himself a supporter of the race. Not to be outdone, the parish priests used their pulpit influence to request parishioners to refrain from alcohol on raceday. A Carlow lady farmer, however, took exception to the date. 'That's the day of Borris fair!' she harangued Council officials.

At the end of June, a notice was posted around the entire circuit, and delivered to all local residents. Occupiers of premises on or near the course were warned to 'keep livestock, pigs, dogs, poultry and cattle under proper control, either in farmyards or well-fenced enclosures, during progress of the said race. Any person on the road, or attempting to cross the road during the progress of the race, will imperil not only his own life but that of the driver of the racing motorcar.' An Athy character noted, 'It says nothing about wives!'

Police were to check that all gates were firmly closed and trackside fields cleared of livestock. Vehicles would be permitted to move all day inside the town controls, but only at police discretion. In case of emergency, police would escort medical personnel or clergy across the course. The Royal Irish Constabulary were also to be issued with red flags with which they would warn competitors of any obstruction. The public could only cross the course between the entry and exit race controls.

The people of county Kildare in particular entered enthusiastically into the spirit of the big event. To mark the occasion, a man who was building two houses in Kildare town named one of them 'Gordon House' and the other 'Bennett House.' As enthusiasm grew in the horse racing heartland where anything that moved was the subject of a betting flutter, enterprising locals studied the motor racing form. Visiting motorists were eagerly canvassed. After requesting a tip from Henry Farman in Monasterevin, a prospective punter asked him 'Is there no Irish car to support, then?' The Frenchman replied 'No. You gave us the road!'

Ireland wouldn't be Ireland, however, without that dissenting voice. The nationalist *Irish People* raced into an aggressive top gear.

> *From the outset, we had no love whatever for the project and these death-dealing machines and their drivers, and the hordes of interested speculators and morbid sightseers who follow in their train to this country. Under healthy conditions of self-regulated National life, what is called the 'Tourist Industry' might be encouraged in Ireland with a modicum of advantage to the people. But, under existing circumstances, the advent of these flittering crowds of vulgar, irreligious and soulless foreigners amongst our people produces no lasting good, and is responsible for much permanent demoralisation.*
>
> *The real truth is that no English County Council would undertake the responsibility of keeping a clear road for the potential suicidals and murderers, who are to risk their own lives and imperil the lives of others in order to advantage the output of the English, French, German and American manufacturing firms.*

The *People* darkly concluded:

> *For the better part of a whole day, 100 miles of Irish roadways will be reserved for the motorist. Happily, the landlords of a past generation have seen to it that the country selected has been almost depopulated, so that if the people who remain are wise enough to keep a civil distance from the roads which they maintain, the casualties may be restricted to the visitors!*

Nationalists with long memories supported the Gallic competitors. They recalled that country's assistance during the 1798 rebellion, when a detachment of French had routed the English at Castlebar. A correspondent wrote:

> *Frenchmen were concerned in 'races' in this country before they ever saw the plains of Kildare. They took part in the very historic 'Races of Castlebar'.*

*Then the English proved themselves the speedier by far. Try as he could, General Humbert failed to overtake the sprinters who ran away with General Lake. On the present occasion, let us hope that the situation will be reversed, and that each Gaul will manage to show a clean pair of heels to his Saxon rivals!*

*Selwyn Edge impressed with preparations.*

The biggest threat to the Irish race came not from nationalists or anti-motoring sentiment, but from the sport itself. The first shadow was cast by Count Eliot Zborowski's death in the La Turbie hillclimb. The dashing Pole's cufflinks jammed the throttle open and he crashed fatally (his son, Louis of the monster 23-litre 'Chitty-Chitty Bang-Bang' fame, was said to be wearing the same cufflinks when he was killed at Monza 20 years later). It was Count Zborowski who first suggested that the British team cars should be painted green, as a mark of respect to the host country, since which time green has remained the official British racing colour.

An even bigger disaster was the May 1903 Paris-Madrid race, which had to be terminated at Bordeaux after at least ten drivers and spectators perished in accidents. The French were rightly proud of their immense contribution to motoring and motorsport. Their organisation, however, proved woefully inadequate for the totally unprecedented interest in the race. None had predicted the chaos of the 300,000 crowd at the early-morning Versailles start, nor the estimated two million spectators who lined the route to Bordeaux. Charles Jarrott recorded the horror of that event.

*The crowd hadn't the least idea what motor car speed was. The road from the start was fast and straight for three or four miles — but it was packed solid with people. You could see the crowds dividing up, some going one side and some the other. It was a ghastly sight.*

On the open roads, where drivers sometimes negotiated seventeenth century coach bridges, the nightmare grew. Jarrott remembered:

*... the long never-ending white ribbon stretching away to the horizon; the holding of a bullet directed to that spot on the sky-line where earth and heaven met; fleeting glimpses of towns and dense masses of people — mad people, insane and reckless, holding themselves in front of the bullet to be ploughed and cut and maimed to extinction, evading the inevitable at the last moment in frantic haste; overpowering relief, as every mass was passed and every chance of catastrophe escaped.*

Not all the drivers escaped. Racing through the suburb of Coignieres side by side, the American Terry tried to forge ahead of the Belfast pair, Leslie Porter and co-driver Willie Nixon. Terry's Mercedes burst its petrol tank after hitting the pavement and Porter had to drive through a stream of liquid flames, when escaping petrol was ignited by the red-hot exhaust.

It was to be but a temporary reprieve. Further down the road, the Irishmen were suddenly confronted by a sharp turn at the temporarily unmanned Bonneval level-crossing. Their Wolseley crashed and caught fire, killing Nixon and consuming the 7,000 francs which Porter had given him for safekeeping in case he was killed. Drivers Marcel Renault and Lorraine Barrow and his mechanic perished in separate accidents.

The government stopped the race at Bordeaux. This marked the end of the great city-to-city events, the distinctive hallmark of early motor-racing. Henceforth, most races would be held on safer, more controllable circuits, of which the Athy Gordon Bennett course was one of the first.

The *Yellow Press* waxed eloquent: 'Motor Massacre', 'The Petrol Death', 'Motor-car Age or Motor Carnage?' Selwyn Edge, however, laid the blame fairly and squarely on the inadequate French organisation. Despite noting Irish motorsport's first fatality, the *Freeman's Journal* also waded in vigorously against 'the English sensation-mongers in the press and out of it, who seem to have gone clear mad on the subject of motoring and motorsport.' The paper wisely pointed out that there was absolutely no comparison between the race for 220 cars over 1,000 miles of open roads and the Irish competition for 12 national cars over a 100-mile course, which would be patrolled by a force of 7,000 police.

*French artist Montaut's depiction of Fernand Gabriel winning the last city-to-city race, which was stopped at Bordeaux.*

Motoring media quickly pointed out that many sports were more dangerous yet provoked little censure. Three jockeys had already died in Britain that year. And what about hunting, shooting, yachting, mountaineering — and even the sedate but frequently disfiguring game of cricket? The Paris–Madrid disaster led to the banning of racing in France. But not even the anti-motoring French group's cable asking King Edward to ban the event could stop the Irish juggernaut.

Course improvements brought much-needed employment and money to many localities. Steamrollers snorted and flints flew. Grittily-earned pints were downed as contractors and workers redoubled their efforts to ensure the best possible road conditions for the big event. The *Freeman's Journal* reiterated 'The contest on the second of July promises to be as safe as viewing an express train go by. In Ireland there is not now, nor never was, the slightest whisper of disapproval of the race.'

*Winding road between Carlow and Maganey. Photograph was commissioned by Mercedes driver, Baron de Caters, before the race.*

# Final Race Preparations

*Exemplary organisation — teams chosen — Americans' European debut — fire destroys German entries*

As Ireland prepared to greet the Gordon Bennett cars, arduous days and nights were spent on refining the race organisation. This would later receive unanimous praise from competitors and the representatives of overseas clubs. The essential timing and race control systems were prepared and supervised by the ACGBI's Captain Robert Phillips, whose official timekeepers were Pembroke Coleman, T.H. Wollen and V. Tampier of the French Automobile Club. The most complicated ever used, the timekeeping has been acknowledged as inaugurating the modern era of accurate recording. No fewer than eighty four silver chronographs were used, twelve for each of the seven control points and one for each competitor. Sheltered by a weather-board, a large dial clock was also provided at each entrance and exit control for the benefit of the drivers.

The controls were situated at Athy, Carlow, Castledermot, Kildare, Kilcullen, Monasterevin and Stradbally. Each had a staff of 26, consisting of a head marshal (green badge), three control stewards as personal assistants (green stripes), a starter to send off the cars (white badge), three timekeepers (red badges), two registrars to record the laps (blue badges), a press steward to inform the media (yellow badge), and fifteen fearless cyclists to guide competitors through the neutralised zones to the exit control (green armbands and gold badges). Volunteer motorcyclists would carry despatches and transfer the all-important time vouchers from Kilcullen to the timekeepers' headquarters at Ballyshannon.

Each control was marked by two high poles which held a red banner with the title 'Automobile Club' across the road. Drivers had to stop between the white lines which were painted twenty feet apart under the banner. Anyone who overshot had to reverse into the correct position. Competitors were allowed to eat or drink between the entrance and exit controls, but not to replenish their cars. All adjustments or repairs had to be carried out in their own time, outside the control areas.

Timing started immediately a car parked between the white lines. The clock was then locked in a wooden box, which was carried by the cyclist who escorted the car to the exit control. Here the clock was stopped as soon as the driver departed, the cyclist then returning it to the original control. As the competitor left, a voucher recording his total stationary time was deposited in a special pouch by the starter. When the driver reached Kilcullen control, the voucher was removed and sent by motorcycle courier to the timekeeping headquarters at Ballyshannon. The original idea for dockets to be sent directly from each control was discarded as being too slow, drivers being likely to complete a circuit before times were received from outlying controls.

The length of time a car was held in a control varied from one minute at Kilcullen Cross, to three minutes at Monasterevin, five at Castledermot, six at Stradbally, eight at Kildare, ten at Carlow and twelve at Athy East and West controls. The scheduled control delays of 57 minutes for each course were to be deducted from competitors' gross times at the end of each lap. An interval of at least two minutes was to be maintained between the dispatch of each car. If two drivers arrived simultaneously, exit priority was to be given to the faster one. At the Kilcullen Cross junction control, the head marshal was to give each competitor a card to remind him of which circuit he was to take: red to turn right for the eastern course, green to go straight on for the western course.

An electrical timing system was established to record speeds over a Flying Mile which ended at the Ballyshannon club enclosure. An elaborate signalling system alerted competitors to approaching bends and controls. A small triangular green flag warned a driver to go cautiously for 440 yards, while a large green one denoted a corner 300 yards ahead. An additional red pendant underlined a particularly dangerous bend. A red flag warned a competitor to stop immediately. The police were also issued with red flags to halt competitors in case of a course obstruction.

As well as the 7,000 police, the circuit was to be controlled by over a thousand volunteer members of the local councils and the automobile club. There was a head officer for each ten miles, which was further divided into quarter-mile sections patrolled by county council members or local residents. Their duty was to see that none of the public or stray animals encroached on the circuit. Every junction was guarded by RIC members, with wire or heavy ropes blocking each side-road and street. Altogether, 270 roads were fenced off for the race, and each gateway, laneway and stile boasted its own sentinel. 'We will show the French how to organise a race!' promised indefatigable *Motor News* editor, R. J. Mecredy.

As raceday approached, interest focused on the competitors and their incredible machines. The world's most skilled and fearless drivers were coming to Ireland, men who had participated in those great city-to-city marathons. And they were bringing the world's fastest road vehicles — machines which could devour a whole mile in a minute! Mors and Panhard cars were chosen to represent France, while special trials were held in England and the U.S, to determine their teams.

But the Gordon Bennett Cup event was to be threatened by one final catastrophe. Just weeks before the race, a huge fire destroyed the Daimler factory at Cannstatt. The conflagration consumed the German team cars whose preparation had almost been completed. The loss of the Gordon Bennett machines was a bitter blow, so much of the company's hopes had rested on them. Mercedes' future, however, was not as important to Irish organisers as the absence of a German team. With little time remaining, it looked as if only a depleted entry of three nations would contest the event.

The disaster, however, led to unprecedented international co-operation to save both Mercedes and the Irish race. *Autocar* magazine appealed to owners of 60 hp machines to lend them to the Germans for the race. At one time, it looked as if an Irish-owned car would participate, as Alfred Harmsworth agreed to lend his Mercedes. But in the end, three almost-new 60 hp touring cars were tracked down by the resourceful Champs Elysses dealer and former racing cyclist, Charley Lehmann. These were owned by Baron de Caters, James Foxhall-Keene and the bearded Paris-based American millionaire, Clarence Gray Dinsmore. It took ardent persuasion by both Lehmann and Baron de Caters before Dinsmore finally agreed to let 'that wild man, Jenatzy' drive his car. With less than a fortnight to run, the Gordon Bennett Cup was back on course!

*Forceful Emil Jellinek persuaded Daimler to race.*

Mercedes owed a singular debt to the impetuous and egocentric 50-year old Czech, Emil Jellinek, Austria's Honorary Consul in Nice. He was one of the few who were happier that Mercedes would race with proven 60 hp cars, rather than the new 90 hp version, which he felt was not yet sufficiently developed. Though he chose the warm Cote d'Azur as his home, Jellinek's trademark was the white pith helmet he wore constantly to protect himself from 'the murderous sun!' It was his sale of over 100 cars to the Riviera rich which really put the Daimler company on its wheels.

And without the forceful former stockbroker, who as 'Herr Mercedes' had made Daimler's 1900 Nice competition debut, they would have already abandoned racing. After their driver Wilhelm Bauer had been killed in the La Turbie hillclimb, Jellinek blamed the crash on faulty design. He advised the company to continue racing, insisting 'Victories will bring world fame. The winning make will be bought, and will always be bought. If you do not enter racing, the conclusion will be drawn that you are unable to enter. It would be commercial suicide to abandon racing.'

Jellinek persuaded Wilhelm Maybach and Paul Daimler to construct the innovative 1901 Mercedes. Its low centre of gravity, honeycomb radiator, gate-change gearbox, sharply-inclined steering wheel and pressed steel frame set the standard for all future cars, even into the ensuing millennium. The new machine was called after Jellinek's eleven-year-old daughter, Mercedes. 'Such a beautiful car should bear a beautiful name,' he convinced the Daimler hierarchy. Unlike the Teutonic 'Daimler' label, the name also conveniently overcame anti-German prejudice in the huge French market (it was only 30 years since the bitter Franco-Prussian war). From 1902 onwards, Mercedes was officially registered as the title for the entire range of Daimler vehicles.

The twelve Irish Gordon Bennett competitors were to drive six different makes of automobile. Though Mercedes had yet to score a major success, the company opened 1903 by breaking records at Nice and the La Turbie hillclimb and was hungry for further honours. Its three borrowed Irish cars were swiftly taken to Cannstatt, where they were prepared as thoroughly as if they were factory racers. Each stripped down tourer was converted to standard Sprint bodywork, with a low-backed pedestal seat and aluminium cowl and hood. Though time was at a premium, the cars emerged like purposeful Phoenixes from the flames and were arguably the most stylish in the race. They featured sloped dashboards, pressed-steel chassis, 9.2-litre engines with low-tension Bosch magneto ignition, and transmission brakes which were cooled from large offside water tanks. And so keen were the drivers Jenatzy and Baron de Caters to safeguard their newly-prepared machines, that they locked them in a Paris cellar while en route to Ireland!

*'Such a beautiful car should bear a beautiful name' — the original Mercedes.*

The most successful of the 1903 race entrants was Panhard, which was selected to represent France together with Mors. The marque won most of the early motor races until challenged by Mors, which had dominated the recent Paris–Madrid in which all three Panhards, driven by Farman, Rene de Knyff and Henri Fournier, had broken down. The Irish race would be of immense importance to Panhard in recovering the ground it had lost, and staff worked hard to prepare its cars for 2 July. These featured the same 13,672cc engine size used in the 1902 Gordon Bennett Cup event, but they had progressed to mechanically-operated side valves in a T-head. With a pronounced rake to the front, the 80 hp machines boasted conventional front suspension with semi-elliptic springs. For the first time, Panhard used pressed steel frames, instead of the original wooden ones, and the car's untidy tubular radiator was now encased in a metal shell.

Emile Mors wisely concentrated on construction, after breaking his collarbone in the 1898 Paris–Bordeaux. Two city-to-city successes swiftly propelled his cars into the limelight in 1901. Following Gabriel's resounding Paris–Madrid triumph the company was confident of success in Ireland. Its lone Dauphin car used a pressed steel chassis for the first time, and a bigger and longer-stroke 70 hp engine than in the 1902 race. Like Panhard, the Mors featured mechanically-operated inlet valves, but it was one step ahead with inlet-over-exhaust layout. The car was more streamlined than its competitors with its upturned-boat style bodywork. Paris–Berlin winner Henri Fournier, who was originally nominated as one of the drivers for the Irish race, explained its aerodynamic properties to a bemused James Joyce. 'The car is short in front, like a fish's head, and then long, like its tail. After you break the air, it rushes in behind and pushes you, so you must have the car short in front, and long behind.'

Selwyn Edge's 1902 success ensured two of the English team places for Napiers driven by himself and the experienced Charles Jarrott. Eliminating tests were held at Welbeck and Dashwood Hill to decide the final representative. Dennis Brothers and Wolseley were to field new cars, but in the end only a Star driven by Joseph Lisle and the Napiers of Charles Rolls and J.W. Stocks appeared. The former cyclist Rolls showed great speed before valve trouble intervened and Stocks was selected after being quickest both ways over the standing mile. The tests highlighted the handicap under which British manufacturers worked. With neither race track nor any local competitions, the trials took place surreptitiously on open roads in the early hours of the morning — and the speeds in excess of 50 mph were highly illegal!

Having made their competition debut only in 1901, Napier cars were fledglings compared to the more experienced Mors and Panhard marques. For the Irish event, Edge reserved for himself the entirely new K5 car, which was credited with 80 bhp. Feeling this was too powerful for the Irish roads, he belatedly opted for the same 45 model driven by J.W. Stocks and Charles Jarrott. He was to change his mind again just before the race, with fateful results. The 13.7 litre Napiers used shaft drive and a three-speed gearbox, and featured the new modification of a Mercedes-style honeycomb radiator.

Two trials were held in Long Island to determine the U.S. representation. C.W. Matheson and future aviator Harry Harkness were rumoured to be building special machines, but only Percy Owen in a Winton and Louis Mooers in a Peerless appeared for the opening test. The Harkness arrived but failed to start the second trial, while both the Peerless machines presented by Mooers also malfunctioned. The American Automobile Club was rebuked by the media for the fiasco, which was hardly a good omen for either the success of the Gordon Bennett or the future of the American auto industry. Louis Mooers in a Peerless, and Percy Owen and Alexander Winton in Wintons were eventually chosen for the race.

*Alexander Winton's 'flying bedstead.'*

The American cars were the least race-proven race entries. The low-slung Wintons were long wooden-framed machines, which Kildare spectators dubbed 'flying bedsteads.' Percy Owen's smaller model boasted a four-cylinder 8.5-litre engine and a two-speed gearbox with direct top gear, which claimed 40 hp. The lower gear was discarded for the race. The car carried fifteen gallons of petrol — and eight of water, as it constantly overheated.

Alexander Winton's larger car was powered by two four-cylinder in-line engines bolted together to form an even thirstier straight-eight 17-litre unit, the biggest in the race! It claimed 80 bhp at 1000 rpm, but had only one forward speed (later U.S. Sprint successes underlined its potential, after Winton had discovered that gear numbers were as important as those of cylinders). The sole Peerless entry designed and driven by Louis Mooers was a more European-looking machine, with a solid steel frame, a tubular radiator like Panhard and three forward gears. Its 4-cylinder engine featured mechanically operated inlet valves and T-head layout, and the advanced feature of full-pressure lubrication via a crankshaft-driven pump.

Like Napier, the Peerless and Winton cars employed shaft drive. The Mercedes, Mors and Panhard machines still featured dangerously exposed side chains. All the competing cars were wooden-wheeled with pneumatic tyres and carried numbers twelve inches high to facilitate identification. The British team used Dunlop tyres, the French sported Michelins, the Germans Clipper Continentals (eventually), and the Americans, Goodridge Clippers which were practically Dunlop, but made in the US. With the national teams chosen, it was only left to select the drivers for the big event.

*The Mercedes 60 hp racer which was to win the race.*

# 7 Daredevils and the Red Devil — The Drivers

World's best represent six nations — de Knyff, hero of city-to-city marathons — Paris–Madrid victor Gabriel — record-breaker 'Red Devil' Jenatzy

While there was no doubt of Mercedes representing Germany, controversy and drama soon enveloped the country's selection of drivers. Rigid class distinction ruled Germany's Automobile Club. It refused the nominations of the experienced Otto Hieronymus and Wilhelm Werner. Not *hochwohlgeborene* high-birth Club members, these Mercedes employees were considered to be players rather than gentlemen (Selwyn Edge and Rene de Knyff were also professionals, but racing executives as opposed to factory floor sweats!).

Rather than compromise, the unbending German officials preferred outsiders of suitable rank to lower-caste locals. Charles Rolls and Baron de Crawhez were at one stage under consideration before the Club finally accepted Baron de Caters, James Foxhall-Keene and Camille Jenatzy. Gentlemen these may have been — but not one of them was German!

Unlike the cars which had to be manufactured entirely in each of the three nations they represented, there was nothing in the regulations as to where the drivers should have been conceived or born! The 1903 Gordon Bennett competitors came from six different countries. And just as none of the German team was born in that country, the French entry included an English and a Belgian-born driver, while the US team leader was Scottish. Four drivers had competed in earlier Gordon Bennett Cup races: Selwyn Edge, Camille Jenatzy, Rene de Knyff and Alexander Winton.

Henry Farman of the French team was the English-born son of the wealthy London *Standard* correspondent, Thomas Farman, who had made Paris his home. His father had known leading artists of the time including the controversial Impressionists, and Henry's first ambition was to be a painter. A restless energetic man, Henry won several French tandem cycling championships with his brother Maurice. But his passion for speed inevitably led him from cycle racing to car competition. As persevering as he was fast, he had many times nursed sick cars to the finish. He won the heavy car class of the 1902 Paris–Vienna race, which incorporated that year's Gordon Bennett Cup. He retired from the Paris–Madrid, after Marcel Renault was fatally injured just ahead of him. A fast but thoughtful driver, 29-year old Farman was to make a name for himself in the Irish race.

*Former cycle racing champion, the elegant Henry Farman.*

The youngest Irish competitor was 23 year-old Fernand Gabriel, whose shy, softly-spoken and courteous manner made him an unlikely racing driver. Of less than average height and with clear far-seeing eyes, the Breton became a consistently competitive driver following his first 1899 Tour de France Voiturettes class success at the age of 20. He overwhelmed the opposition in the foggy 1902 hillclimb at La Turbie, where Zborowski later died. Second in the 1902 Circuit des Ardennes after a race-long duel with Charles Jarrott, his 1903 Paris–Madrid race win ensured him a special place in the pantheon of motorsport heroes. Through the searing heat and blinding dust, he overtook almost one hundred other competitors to reach Bordeaux half an hour ahead of his nearest rival — at an average speed of over 65 mph! His mechanic in that event was Mariage, who was also to race with him in Ireland.

The heavily-bearded patriarchal Rene de Knyff was the *doyen* of motorsport's early heroes. 'The finest in the world!' said fellow-racer Baron Henri de Rothschild, though this title was now threatened by team-mates Farman and Gabriel. Born in Belgium in 1864, de Knyff moved to Paris where he managed his cycle-racing brother and became involved with the leading *Revue des Sports* cycling journal. An early convert to automobilism, his enthusiasm and management skills quickly gained him a directorship with the Panhard-Levassor company, whose many technical innovations he tested in the white heat of racing. Unlike Camille Jenatzy who drove any car that was offered to him, de Knyff ever only raced Panhards. And in contrast to his impetuous compatriot, the Panhard exponent was a cool and calculating driver whose motto was 'always finish'.

Fourth on his 1897 Nice debut, de Knyff scored his first big success in the following year's Paris–Bordeaux race. He then won the 1,350-mile 1899 Tour de France and Belgium's first event, the Spa–Bastogne–Spa. He took the 1901 Pau Circuit de Sud-East race and the Nice–Marseilles–Nice — despite being hit by another driver before the race had even started! He had competed in two previous Gordon Bennett Cup events, retiring while leading Selwyn Edge in the 1902 race.

Unlike many of his rivals, de Knyff was never involved in a racing accident during his distinguished career. At a time when opportunities for chicanery abounded, it was his sportsmanship and organisational skills which helped international motorsport to develop along more professional lines. And, according to Charles Jarrott, de Knyff was not only a mine of information on technical matters and race routes, he could also be relied on to find the best cigars, the best champagne and the most reliable local wines! The naturalised Frenchman was to drive in Ireland with his mechanic Aristides, who was widely regarded as the greatest of the early race technicians.

Representing America, Louis P. Mooers was a talented designer and engineer with the Peerless Car Company. He was an experienced test driver, but, unlike Alexander Winton, he had no experience of racing apart from the abortive American Gordon Bennett trials. He designed the four-cylinder car which he drove in Ireland (and which subsequently established many American speed records). Team-mate Percy Owen was the New York manager of the Winton Motor Company. His bright cheery disposition was to make him a big hit with 1903 Gordon Bennett spectators, though one correspondent described him as 'looking somewhat young and fragile for his task.' Though the Americans lacked the experience of their European rivals, 28-year old Owen won the 1902 Long Island 100-mile race and he also established American speed records.

Regarded by many as the father of the American auto industry, the oldest race entrant was the calm and confident 43-year old Alexander Winton. Son of a Glasgow blacksmith, he had trained as a Clydeside marine engineer before emigrating to the US in 1878. He founded a bicycle company in Cleveland, Ohio, and progressed to motor wagon assembly in 1897, advertising his cars with the slogan 'Away with the whip!'

Two years later, he drove a Winton car from New York to Chicago at 17.6 mph. At the time of the Irish Gordon Bennett event, one of his machines was well on its way to completing the first-ever US coast-to-coast crossing by car. Though he had competed in the opening 1900 Gordon Bennett Cup, retiring with wheel damage, Winton's racing experience was mainly confined to tracks. He raced against Henry Ford at Grosse Point and won at Long Island's Brighton Beach in 1902. Two months before his Irish appearance, he set up an American record of 68 mph over one mile at the first Daytona Speed Trials. It was his brash challenge to the Frenchman Fernand Charron which led to the instigation of the Gordon Bennett series.

The three English team members had competed against each other many times on two wheels. The most successful was de Dion Bouton's London agent, the wax-moustached J.W. Stocks, who was English 25-mile champion in 1893. He won the 100-Kilometre World Cycling Championship four years later and also became the first person to ride thirty miles paced in one hour. Progressing to motorcycles, he made the earliest motor tricycle run from John O'Groats to Land's End, after which he toured Ireland by tricycle in 1900. He gave special demonstrations at Derry's Brandywell and the newly concreted Ballymena track, where he covered five miles in under ten minutes. Selwyn Edge described his team-mate as 'one of the finest drivers of either racing or touring cars who ever lived.' Though he lacked car racing experience, 33-year old Stocks had competed in many reliability trials and shown speed and dash at the English qualifying trials to take the remaining team place from Charles Rolls.

Frequently described as the archetypal Englishman for his courage, determination and consistently stiff upper lip, Selwyn Francis Edge was in fact born in Sydney in 1868. His family moved shortly afterwards to England, where he first made his name by establishing cycling records for the runs from London to Brighton and York. In 1887, he completed 100 miles in 5 hours and 6 minutes at Herne Hill track. He finished third in the Paris–Bordeaux marathon and, after progressing to motorcycles, returned there for the 1899 tricycle event. His pioneering efforts ensured that he became one of the first British victims of road rage, surviving several attacks by angry carriage drivers!

In 1901, Edge persuaded engineer David Napier, father of fellow-cyclist Montague Napier, to build him a special car for the Gordon Bennett race. The machine proved too powerful for its tyres but a year later Edge steered a more modest 30 hp machine to Great Britain's historic success in the Gordon Bennett section of the gruelling Paris–Vienna event. With his flair for publicity and an unquenchable belief in the value of international racing, he did more than any other individual to promote motoring in England during the early 1900's. Black-browed, utterly fearless and rarely smiling, Edge was too cautious to be a front-line racer. But it was his true grit in that 1902 race which, after those three sleepless nights, wrested the international trophy from the French and ensured the staging of the momentous 1903 Irish event.

'Few ordinary men have loved any personal thing as I loved the never-ending road!' Charles Jarrott wrote lyrically. Born in 1877, he was a successful cyclist until he forsook a promising legal career for the thrills of motorsport. He raced tricycles for three years, then progressed to four wheels and finished

*The first US team to race in Europe.*

*Louis Mooers*

*Percy Owen*

*Alexander Winton*

tenth in the 1901 Paris–Berlin event. He took second place in the 1902 Circuit du Nord with his mechanic, George du Cros. The Dubliner also accompanied Jarrott on the 1902 Paris–Vienna race, in which they finished twelfth with only one gear remaining, no clutch, no exhaust and a broken chassis which they had repaired with furniture purloined from their hotel. Fortified by a bottle of champagne from an enthusiastic supporter, Jarrott scored the first international success by a British driver in the 1902 Circuit des Ardennes. One of his finest races was the ill-fated Paris–Madrid, in which he drove brilliantly despite a damaged front wheel, to finish third behind Gabriel and Salleron. Noted for his speed, courage and attention to detail, Jarrott was the antithesis of his cooler more calculating team-mate Edge. He frequently reiterated 'No sport was worth a rap that didn't contain an element of risk. Why, risk was the spice of the whole game!'

James Foxhall-Keene added a dash of Celtic zest and charm to the German team. Born at Long Island in 1870, his equally colourful father was an adventurer who, by wiser investment, recovered the California Gold Rush fortune he had lost on earlier rash speculation. The family raised thoroughbred horses in Kentucky and 'Foxie' Keene became one of America's best known steeplechasers and polo players. Riding accidents led to a broken collarbone and many hospitalisations before he tried the comparatively safer sport of motor racing. A daring and fast driver, he crashed his Mors in the 1901 Paris–Berlin race, but progressed doggedly to sixteenth before finally yielding to mechanical problems. He was introduced to Mercedes by his friend, Emil Jellinek.

*James Foxhall-Keene in his Mercedes.*

Chivalry and sportsmanship were the distinguishing hallmarks of the handsome 28-year old millionaire racer, Baron Pierre de Caters. His motorsport, motorboat and aviation feats were to make him a national hero in his native Belgium — although his immediate aristocratic family was less than enthralled with such sport involvement. A cool and self-possessed competitor, the Baron drove many different makes of cars in the early road races. He finished third for Mors in the 1901 Nice–Salon–Nice event and, the following year, set a new world record of 75 mph at Ostend. His wife unsuccessfully tried to dissuade him from racing in Ireland, following the Paris–Madrid disaster. De Caters' mechanic was to be Frenchman Gustave Girard, who had accompanied fellow Mercedes driver Hieronymous in the same Paris–Madrid event.

*Baron de Caters in his Mercedes.*

On a showery 1899 April morning as dark storm clouds banked overhead, a deceptively silent torpedo-like machine sped down the straight road of Acheres Park, north west of Paris. The blue wind-cheater rushed past spectators with an unnerving swish of its four tiny rubber wheels, leaving tracks that swiftly converged on the horizon like a railway line. Jutting incongruously out of the aerodynamic car like a chick breaking out of its shell, was its bearded Belgian designer, Camille Jenatzy. He raced into the history books as the first person to drive at a mile a minute and 100 kilometres per hour, a 65.79 mph (105.85 kph) record that was not to be beaten for three years. It was his third time to hold the world land speed record. The machine's name, *La Jamais Contente*, aptly expressed its designer's restless and excitable personality (though some ungraciously suggested it was called after his allegedly Xantippean wife!).

Born in 1868 to an immigrant Hungarian family who had founded Belgium's first rubber factory, the short, leanly-built and red-bearded Jenatzy was typical of many racing drivers; a gentleman off the track, a devil on it! A contemporary wrote 'None presented such a terrifying appearance in a car.

*Camille Jenatzy in Mercedes he'd driven from Germany.*

Although reckless, daring and exciting to the utmost degree when racing, a more meek and mild-mannered individual when off the car could not be imagined.'

Another former racing cyclist, Jenatzy was a civil engineer before he turned to motor manufacturing. He entered motor racing with sprint cars which he built to publicise his electric cabs. He won the first-ever hillclimb in 1898 at Chanteloup and was seventh in the following year's Paris–St Malo race, despite losing time when he gave first aid to an injured competitor. The landmark record-breaker was one of the fastest drivers in the Paris–Madrid race, having progressed to third place before a fly in the carburettor cost him three hours and thirteen places.

One of motorsport's first colourful characters and a consistently fearless driver who pioneered the controlled four-wheel slide, the Belgian always raced on the limit. Charles Jarrott recalled passing the wreckage of his car in the 1902 Circuit des Ardennes.

> *The motor and one part of the frame were on one side, the back axle and wheels a hundred yards up on the other side. A little further on, I came across Jenatzy in a small car, proceeding back to the control, and as he stood up and waved I caught a glimpse of a red beard, a bloodstained face and a bandaged head, a picture thoroughly characteristic of his reputation!*

The Belgian was lucky to escape from that accident with just the loss of his right thumb, a handicap which did little to inhibit his totally committed driving style.

Like Gabriel and de Knyff, Jenatzy was accompanied to Ireland by his Paris–Madrid mechanic, Fritz Walker. Jenatzy raced in Ireland under a shadow; he had earlier been given a suspended prison sentence for his part in an accident which claimed the life of a young French woman. Following his Paris–Madrid misfortune, the Mercedes driver was anxious to do well. But he had misgivings about the circuit which, after an early reconnaissance, he described as one of the most difficult he had seen. The Belgian wore light waterproof clothes which billowed behind him and sometimes enveloped his head, giving him according to the *Morning Post* 'the impression of a satyr.' His excitable nature ensured that he quickly became a favourite of Irish race spectators. They were to give him a rousing welcome and a new title, 'The Red Devil.'

'They shall not pass!' *The formidable English team of Stocks, Jarrott and Edge pictured in Dublin's Phoenix Park.*

# 8  Teams, Aristocracy and Fashions Arrive

Thousands welcome teams — drivers' view of course — Percy French 'Now we sing a swifter steed' — hotel overcharging — Gordon Bennett!

The Gordon Bennett teams arrived in Ireland at the end of June. Irish wanderers had originally traversed Europe as pilgrims, missionaries, scholars and professional soldiers — and a good job for western civilisation that they had! For it was Irish monks such as Adamnan, Dicuil and Johannes Scotus who had brought knowledge and scholarship to the courts of Charlemagne and Charles the Bald. Armed only with walking sticks, water bottles and leather satchels holding laboriously copied manuscripts, their zeal and learning helped dissipate the darkness which the Barbarian destruction of the Roman Empire had drawn over Europe. But now, the big motor race was bringing modern Europe and the latest technology to Ireland, and thousands hastened to greet the continental teams at Dublin port.

The French didn't let them down. A veritable *Who's Who* of early automoblism sailed into Alexandria Dock on board the three-masted *Ferdinand de Lesseps* steamer, which had been specially chartered by a syndicate of Parisian manufacturers. Blue-bloused mechanics lined the bow of the ship which was crammed with tools and spare-parts, a floating motor workshop. Among the 145 passengers were constructors Emile Mors and A. Panhard, and the tyre maker Andre Michelin. The aristocracy included banker Baron Henri de Rothschild, French Automobile Club president, Baron de Zuylen de Nyevelt, the fencing champion, Duc de Arian, Belgian racer Baron de Forest, and Circuit des Ardennes winner Baron de Crawhez, who had just finished fourth in the Paris–Madrid.

Other notable racing drivers included Jean Salleron and the American amateur John B. Warden, second and fifth respectively in the same race, Maurice Farman, record-breaker Louis Rigolly and future Gordon Bennett winner, Leon Thery. A cheer went up when the French spotted Paris–Madrid winner Gabriel, who had preceded them to Dublin. As well as the official Mors and Panhard team cars and visitors' tourers, the ship also brought such exotic machinery as Rigolly's giant Gobron-Brillie, de Forest's Mors, and Prunel and Decauville racing cars, which would contest the speed trials.

The first Irishman aboard the ship to welcome the French was the ubiquitous Harvey du Cros. He was accompanied by his champion cycling progeny George, William and Harvey Junior, who by then were gainfully involved with both Dunlop and Panhard. Delighted to see some of the French sporting green caps and ties as a complement to the host country, onlookers responded vociferously when du Cros Senior called 'Three cheers for the first French racers to land on Irish soil!' Further acclaim greeted the first car to be slung over the side. Enraptured by their welcome, the French handed out cigarettes to the adults and 'French pennies' to the younger gamins.

'Are they cars or canoes?' spectators asked, as they studied the streamlined Mors machines. Gabriel and Salleron, however, wasted little time with the celebrations. No sooner were two of the Mors swung overboard, than they asked smokers to extinguish their cigarettes. They quickly filled their cars with highly inflammable motor-naphta. They then clipped on their goggles, and sped down the Liffey quays towards monastic Kildare in the projectiles which they had so recently guided to first and second places in the last of the great city-to-city races.

In addition to its insurance-nightmare complement of star drivers, cars and aristocracy, the *Ferdinand de Lesseps* also brought the very latest Parisian fashion to Dublin! The smartly dressed lady passengers attracted almost as much attention as the cars, as they paraded their couture around the city in the days prior to the race. They later went on to make an equally dramatic impact at the Naas weighing-in. While a French social columnist lamented that so many of the fashionable folk and motorists had deserted Paris for the wilder shores of Ireland, the Dublin media rejoiced that the continentals and their cars and costumes had brought a welcome carnival atmosphere to the Irish capital.

The English had already arrived a fortnight earlier, while the Winton team had disembarked at North Wall with their crated cars on 22 June. Louis Mooers' participation got off to an unpropitious start, when it proved

*'Three cheers for the first French racers to land on Irish soil!'*

impossible to unload his car at Queenstown and it had to be taken to Liverpool and then redirected to the North Wall. The Germans came by an equally circuitous route, driving their Mercedes convoy from Cannstatt to Paris and Le Havre, and then again from Southampton to Holyhead. They also brought with them a motor bus and a roomy 'camping-out car.'

Although the French had been liberal with their cigarettes, Dublin dockers subsequently spoke more highly of the English and Americans. One handler explained 'Their tips were most generous, being quite a golden shower.' Other visitors of un-recorded nationality were dismissed as being 'a right shower,' a euphemism for stingy. By a, hopefully, totally un-related coincidence, one of their cars fell from a crane, leading to a £120 claim against the North Western Railway Company!

*Tara via Holyhead — the popular Louis Mooers.*

Accommodation suddenly became a priority as the number of visitors grew. As early as January, property owners near the circuit sensed a bonanza in the making. Some of these were more enterprising than literate. *Motor News* received a letter which read 'Gordon Bennett, Mainger Mouter Arise, Dublin. As you are mainger of mouter arise, I wish u to send me 10 men to loug four 3 days as I have 3 bedsrooms very nise sitin room if you be so kind to let me no.'

For some hoteliers, the event provided an irresistable Golden Egg opportunity which a few shamelessly exploited. One Athy hotel refused to accept bookings at all, preferring to see what it would be offered during race week. Forward-thinking visitors who had agreed prices for houses near the circuit, found that their owners had doubled the prices before race day. According to *Autocar*, 'jarveys unblushingly asked for ten shillings a seat from Athy to Ardscull, while twopenny mineral water cost sixpence in the meanest shebeen.' Thus was born the 'Gordon Bennett!' euphemism for skullduggery and disbelief — an alternative to the Cockney 'Cor Blimey.'

Having been ripped off in Kildare establishment, a disillusioned Scottish scribe sadly wrote, 'Gordon Bennett is a new Irish word for fleece.' Another correspondent wrote of a friend 'whose ideals were shattered in that Gordon Bennett week — who has an Irish hotel bill framed which he intends to hand down to posterity.' An *Irish Cyclist* correspondent was moved to verse:

*Such bills! Such cheques! Great Scott!*
*It filled us all with great alarm*
*To shell out their demands.*
*We like old Erin's open arms*
*But not her open hands!*

The most eloquent answer to grasping hoteliers was provided by an American visitor. He voted with his feet when asked to pay £7 for a room the night before the race. 'I guess you're making a mistake, friend,' he drawled. 'I have more money on me than that!'

The most publicized story of overcharging, however, proved to have been based on a misunderstanding involving none other than Richard Mecredy. He had approached the proprietor of Kilmeade post office for accommodation for his wife. After reiterating that he did not rent rooms, postmaster James Kelly subsequently explained 'I said five or six pounds, intending the answer not as a price for a room but as an intimation that Mrs. Mecredy might look farther.' Sadly, Mecredy's original report received a wider and more damaging airing than the subsequent explanation.

Most local and Dublin hotels in fact heeded the Irish Hotels Proprietors Association's advice on fair prices. They retained normal rates for the duration of the race, though some insisted on a minimum of a four nights' stay. The Association published a list which included Dublin's fashionable Wynn's and Clarence Hotels, where bed and breakfast was available for ten shillings a night. D.J. Brennan's course-side hotel at Kilcullen offered the same rate, including garage shelter.

And as *The Irish Times* London correspondent pointed out, the Irish didn't have a monopoly of overcharging. He recalled the exorbitant prices recently demanded by Londoners for accommodation near the Coronation route! The London and North Western Railway Company took advantage of the race to increase its advertised Holyhead-North Wall fare by fifty shillings at owner's risk and three pounds at company's risk. Some visitors were in fact struck by the honesty of the Irish. A French visitor told his compatriots of the Dublin shirtmaker who could not change a note: 'It's all right, sir. You'll pay me when you are passing.'

The enterprising Richard Mecredy and James Percy set up a camp at the elevated thirteenth-century motte known locally as the Moat of Ardscull. They erected sufficient Bell tents to sleep 600 at a guinea and a half each (almost 1,000 were eventually accommodated), and a grandstand for 300 in an adjoining field for which admission cost half a guinea. A separate tented field was allocated to members of the fair sex. The locals, however, resented this appropriation of what they considered to be public ground. Labourers refused to work and farmers gave them the cold shoulder. When carters refused to deliver anything from Athy railway station, all the tents and equipment had to be brought down directly from Dublin!

Apart from accommodation shenanigans, there was also a question mark over the cost and quality of Irish food. Baron de Crawhez complained of being charged 110 francs for a meal which he said was inferior to what would cost one franc in any French hostelry. The French found the food to be woefully short of Gallic standards and relied heavily on their floating hotel, the *Ferdinand de Lesseps*. They incurred the censure of one scribe, however,

*The Mercedes mob hits town! Baron de Caters stands beside driver Foxhall-Keene, mechanic Willy Luttgen and Clarence Gray Dinsmore, owner of Jenatzy's car.*

when they refused to drink whiskey unless it was from a bottle which they saw being opened. He commented 'Herein the French were unnecessarily fussy, because whatever is wrong with Irish cooking, you can always gamble on the whiskey being drinkable.' Ironically, a short time later, many of the French Automobile Club's top brass succumbed to food poisoning after a Parisian banquet.

Fernand Gabriel stayed briefly at Dublin's Grosvenor Hotel before joining the rest of the Mors team in Loughbrown Lodge at the Curragh. Rene de Knyff, Henry Farman and the Panhard equipe booked into Kilcullen's homely Bardon's Hotel. The German team settled into Athy's newly-opened Leinster Arms establishment, close to the pleasant canal and the river Barrow. America's Winton drivers, Percy Owen and Alexander Winton, staked out Timolin Rectory whose porch they decorated with the Stars and Stripes. Louis Mooers lodged with the Cole family in the former Moone home of eighteenth century Quaker historian and writer Mary Leadbetter.

The British team choose the even more auspicious Rheban Castle, three miles from Athy. Not so much for its ancient associations as the fact that it was the home of former cycle racer Harry Large. As he had lived in Coventry, he could be relied on to serve suitable English food — as well as providing the only modern bathroom in the locality! The English also enjoyed the favouritism of a local RIC man. No doubt with the subversive French in mind, he reassured them 'I'll keep a special eye on your machines, to make sure none of those foreigners damage them!'

It was the French, however, who needed protection, and from some of their own countrymen at that. The Panhard drivers received a series of warning letters, telling them that they might become victims of an English plot. The Gordon Bennett Cupholders were prepared to resort to foul play to prevent the trophy returning to France: French drivers would compete at their peril, car sabotage could not be ruled out.

Henry Farman shrugged the letters off with the insouciance of youth, but Rene de Knyff took them more seriously. Charles Jarrott said afterwards 'Rene de Knyff had more than his share of these communications, and though he only smiled at them, nevertheless I knew he was a little anxious as to what it all meant.' The sporting Englishman reassured the Panhard veteran that there was absolutely no conspiracy of any sort on the part of the English team. Failing to excite a reaction, the letter campaign ceased. Many speculated that the letters were the work of inventive French scribes, hoping for some scandal to spice up their copy.

Thanks to their 'open house' hospitality, the Americans proved the most popular with the locals. Mooers was a particular favourite, being frequently pictured at the helm of a neighbour's donkey and cart. He acquired further popularity points by attending a Dublin nationalist rally. The very Green *Irish People* wrote 'Our good wishes and the good wishes of the vast majority of the Irish people will be with the cheerful and plucky Yankee, Mr. Mooers, whose speech at the Station Hotel, Kingsbridge, on the occasion of Mr. Joseph Devlin's arrival and reception won the hearts of all his hearers.'

The British relaxed by fishing in the Barrow, whose inviting banks washed their backdoor. They explored the neighbourhood and climbed the Rock of Dunamase. Edge, a great believer in physical fitness, trained constantly with the popular Sandows exercise routine, while Stocks and Jarrott played cricket. The trio also made time for a welcoming visit to the Americans. In the evenings they were entertained on Mrs. Large's piano by Ireland's leading light entertainer, Percy French. The 'Mountains of Mourne' composer had penned a cautionary song to mark the Gordon Bennett event:

*And now we sing a swifter steed*
*That's hooting round the land;*
*A mile a minute it can speed,*
*And yet be well in hand;*
*This is a thing that bobbies need*
*To note and understand!*

But the entertainment was for the evenings only. By day, drivers lost no time in learning the racecourse on their swifter steeds. Strictly warned to observe the 12 mph limit, they made as many runs as possible to familiarise themselves with the 91-mile circuit.

The driver's critical perspective was worlds apart from that of the casual onlooker. Where a spectator saw only corners and gradients, the racing driver was concerned with speed and usable space. The criterion was time, where to save it, where to make it, and on these reconnaissance laps to select the optimum deceleration, braking and cornering points. And to note the cambers, the borders which might have to be used in emergency, places where engine and brakes could be rested and where instruments and tyres could be inspected at speed.

The stressful start was followed by a testing one-mile ascent. Listen how the engine responds. Then a gradual descent to tricky Hacklow Corner before the acute southwards change of direction near Old Kilcullen. Both corners sharp and adverse-cambered. A fast tree-lined straight led to Halverstown. Stirring midlands views flashed past unnoticed as drivers checked their instruments for the first time. At eight miles out, the road suddenly narrowed and swept downhill through Ballitore. Two long hills to Timolin taxed engines again, before the sweeping curve into Moone. Another exhilarating one-mile descent burst into the wide straight to Castledermot, 19 miles from the start. Eyes down for those control lines. The gruelling uphill exit gave way to a welcome six-mile decline towards Carlow railway bridge. Any false sense of security was to be sharply interrupted by the fast but ill-concealed left-hand corner at Ballymoon.

Five miles of continuous bends made the northwards Barrow-side run from Carlow (26 miles) one of the course's most demanding sections. A sharp left turn led across high-arched Maganey Bridge, where a stout cottage guarded the equally acute rightward exit. A second tricky bridge tested both brakes and patience again, before the welcome but narrow straight to Athy. Time now to look more carefully at those tyres, and listen more acutely to the engine note.

*Kilcullen — learning the course.*

Another fine high-speed stretch and gentle incline past the Russellstown stand led to the right and left negotiation of the elevated Moat of Ardscull. Lots of spectators here to distract a driver or tempt him into exhibitionism. Then there was only the briefest of stock-taking time, on the rising return past Fontstown church to the startline. The narrowness of the Athy–Kilcullen straight offered little overtaking room, concentration was required to keep machines out of those mocking roadside culverts. The first 40-mile lap of the eastern circuit had been chalked up. Now came the longer western loop, another 50 miles of climbs and corners to be learnt at speed.

The narrow Kilcullen approach led to another uncompromising test of brakes, as one picked up the course card. Between the Scylla and Charybdis of a high wall and a row of inhibiting cottages, a pair of acute double bends led westwards towards the Curragh's welcome airy plains. Top speed here — and a heavy landing if one misjudged a hump. And a firm steering hand, to prevent any wandering on to the ill-defined and unreliable grassy margins.

The unfenced road suddenly dropped down into Kildare's Market Square. Brakes were put on their mettle again by a succession of unforgiving stone railway bridges, the hazardous hallmark double corners of the Victorian railway system. Only light-footed patience going in would allow the optimum exit acceleration for maximum speed down the following straight. The last bridge led to a straight but narrow causeway across five miles of wild-flowered boglands. No time for relaxation here, either. A misplaced wheel would result in swift and permanent ingestion by a Venus's fly-trap of enveloping peat.

The sharp right turn at Mooreabbey Castle slowed cars on the entrance to Monasterevin (21 miles). Then it was smart left turn to cross the meandering Barrow. Stand the machine on its nose again for the acutely-angled Grand Canal bridge. And don't forget that its hidden descent goes in the opposite direction. A long narrow straight led past miles of sighing woodlands to the Ballybrittas ascent. Its flanking hills provided the first silhouetted sighting of the distinctive Rock of Dunamase, under which the cars would soon race

*Wandering donkeys and cows made driving hazardous.*

towards Windy Gap. Ballydavis Cross-roads on the outskirts of Maryboro (32 miles) suddenly marked the end of the straight sections. Its nasty left-hander smartly focused concentration on the yet more arduous sections ahead.

Dunamase led to the speed-tempting but highly dangerous Aghnahilly Bends approach. Then followed the tantalising relief of Stradbally's generously proportioned streets (37 miles). Its exit opened on to the winding ribbon of road which led up to the roof of the midlands at Windy Gap. Hard work for the engine until the top is reached. The pressure was then abruptly transferred from machine to man. Stomachs lightened, the windswept road fell away beneath the wheels. Pray for good brakes again, for the rapid but narrow, swerving four-mile descent past Loughglass to the tippy-toe left-hander of Simmons Cross (44 miles).

A welcome breather followed this most southerly corner with the wide straight run through Ballylynan to Athy and Ballyshannon. That church spire again. Suddenly, it was time to put into practice the lessons learnt on that first exploratory eastern course lap — where late-braking had almost led to disaster, and irrecoverable seconds squandered by slowing too early. And better approach those bumps differently this time, if one is not to be thrown off the road or smashed against a wall.

Napier team leader Selwyn Edge recorded over forty reconnaissance laps. He originally used the smaller Napier before replacing it with the more powerful but untested K5 model. He noted presciently 'It proved to be a good deal faster, and my only fear was that the tyres would not stand the tremendous strain.' Edge's chain failed to stand the strain one evening at Ballylynan, when it was broken by a stone. Locals were amazed to see Jarrott tow the racing machine home behind a little 8 hp de Dion voiturette.

Wandering donkeys, cows, dogs and geese made driving hazardous. The most speed-conscious of the menagerie proved to be the ubiquitous rooks. After sufficient casualties, these learned to go into take-off mode at the merest suspicion of an engine note. Sheep and fowl proved to be slower learners and compensatory shillings changed hands as fur and feathers flew. The conscientious Gabriel one day pulled up his Paris–Madrid Mors outside Kildare police station and deposited five pounds for a sheep he had just killed at the Curragh's Ballymanny Cross. The wild Jenatzy met his match, when he was stopped in his tracks by a formidable matron brandishing a chicken which a preceding motorist had just run over. The Belgian was much amused and he apologised for the four-wheeled assassin before handing the lady two and sixpence and escaping in his racing Mercedes. Hers was but one of an expensive epidemic of slain fowl, which only ceased when drivers learned to take the chickens with them.

Charles Jarrott also had to execute a sudden halt one morning. A constable jumped out from behind a hedge to inform him that he had been driving at 15 mph, three miles over the limit. When the patriotic policeman discovered who the miscreant was, he apologised profusely. He sent him on his way, saying 'Go as fast as you like, and more power to you and your motorcar, as long as you beat the furriners — and dem Germans!'

Interest in the Gordon Bennett rivalled that in the crucial Land Bill, which it was fervently hoped would end landlordism in Ireland. Hundreds of cyclists swarmed around the circuit with the summer bees. Locals happily made tea for the contractors and roadmenders who had smoothed the highways and banished the ubiquitous and hazardous potholes. The national media didn't stint on either coverage or enthusiasm, though sometimes at the price of accuracy. An *Irish Times* journalist described Jenatzy as 'a typical German.' *The Field* rated 'Jenatsky — a formidable driver.'

The noise of hammering and sawing rang across the Kildare plains as spectator stands were erected. Thanks to its multi-lap circuit, the Irish race boasted more stands than any previous international event. The biggest was the official 1,000-seater construction which straddled the circuit beside the Ballyshannon club enclosure, just past the start and finish line at Tippeenan Lane. While Roderic O'Connor was making a name for himself with Paul Gauguin in Brittany, this crude affair of iron beams and wooden planks represented an impressive triumph of strength over beauty. 'Unpicturesque' was its most flattering and printable description. The seating area was devoid of decoration or colour, apart from the flags and providential bunting and the crimson carpeted area which was reserved for the Viceroy and his party. A wooden footbridge allowed Club Enclosure spectators to move from one side of the road to the other.

*The narrow approach to the grandstand under which the cars would race.*

The Thomas Cook agency was in charge of bookings at a guinea a seat, plus an extra guinea for optional use of the club enclosure — which had in fact to be traversed in order to reach the stand! Places were reserved for MPs and members of the local county councils. The keen demand for seats confirmed one envious local's opinion that 'Those that own dem cars has bread buttered on both sides.' A military band was engaged to render suitably exciting and regal music. 'See you at the grandstand, old boy' was a favourite greeting among the upper orders in the week prior to the race.

More modest and less obtrusive structures proliferated around the course. N.P. Walsh offered a 'natural stand' close to the official Ballyshannon edifice, which could be reached at any time during the race and cost only three shillings per person. Thomastown platform, three quarters of a mile along the route, advertised accommodation for five shillings with refreshments available in rooms at the rear of the stand. A stand at Russellstown near Athy cost one shilling extra, while James Kelly offered more modest space for two shillings and sixpence at nearby Youngstown. Between Athy and Ballyshannon, Fontstown stand advertised tea, sandwiches and 'temperance drinks'. A grandstand at the Curragh guaranteed unique views for over three miles, admission five shillings. An offer only bettered at Aughnahilla, opposite the Rock of Dunamase, where admission to the hill cost two and sixpence, and seven and sixpence to the grandstand 'with an unbroken stretch of seven miles visible to the naked eye!'

The pace of off-circuit promotions and peripheral activities rivalled that of the racers. Dublin theatres joined forces to celebrate the Gordon Bennett event. The Empire's 'Motor Week Show' featured singer Marie Kendall and singer-comedienne, Julie Herbert. In addition to the Esmerelda Quartette, the Tivoli offered the daring Whirlwind Cyclists, who looped the loop while suspended in mid-air. Arthur Roberts & Company staged a special variety show at the Theatre Royal. Dubliners were invited to 'come and learn the results of the Motor Race, which will be flashed by the Biograph on to the curtain, the moment news reaches Dublin.'

On a loftier note, the tenor John McCormack was booked to sing at concerts in Athy and Carlow. Sadly, nothing came of the *Leinster Leader*'s appeal to local drama groups 'to stage performances which would impress visitors with the distinctive culture of Ireland.' Some cynics suggested that grasping hoteliers had already achieved this!

While Flanagans of Kilcullen metamorphosed into a 'Motor Bar', many Dublin shops and businesses took advantage of the race to promote their wares. The Swift Cycle Company offered a machine worth eighteen guineas for the person who would correctly forecast the race winner's precise time. Another business offered a fur motor coat for the mechanic of the winning car. Gloves, hats and boots were described as 'specially made for the big race.' Gordon Bennett picnic baskets were widely displayed.

A new phenomenon appeared, the Motoring Shop, selling all the latest gear and accessories. The London Motoring Exhibition launched a special 'Erin' coat made,

> ... from a lovely shade of shamrock-green Irish frieze, with leather yokes of a harmonious green tint. It may be unlined, or lined with very thin leather or silk to taste. Very pretty green metal buttons, ornamented with a motorcar in relief in the centre, complete the decoration. Designed by Lovegrove of 175 Piccadilly, the price is eight guineas.

Race fever wasn't confined to the maccho male motorists. A woman's magazine featured 'A Romance of the Gordon Bennett Race' story by Arabella Kenealy. With such titles to her credit as *The Love of Richard Harris* and *A Semi-Detached Marriage*, she was apparently the Barbara Cartland of the time:

> 'If I win the race,' he said suddenly, in a voice with fire in it, 'what will you give me?'
>
> 'Me blessing,' she returned with roguish eyes. But she was not won so easily, as he found to his cost and ecstasy. The winning of the Gordon Bennett Cup was child's play in comparison.

Gordon Bennett!

# 9 Race-eve Excitement — Cars Weigh in

Dublin 'a petrol-smelling Saturnalia' — Naas weigh-in disputes — German tyres rejected — drivers' premonitions

The focal point of the pre-race activities was the official weighing and checking of the cars at Naas. This attracted thousands of spectators and many foreign visitors. Prior to race week there had been much worried tapping of barometers — 'Irish weather is as unsettled as a baby's bottom,' an Irish writer insisted. But the continentals had brought their climate to Ireland and the teams assembled in glorious sunshine to a chorus of divers tongues.

Townspeople marvelled at the unprecedented number of automobiles, over 200 filled Market Square alone. Another wonder was the furniture lorry with sixteen Terenure enthusiasts, which provided both their catering and rooftop grandstand. But, most of all, spectators revelled in their first opportunity to study the mighty racing machines and their daredevil drivers.

According to the *Kildare Observer*:

> *The ordinary equine was not in it. He and his owner absented themselves and for the time being, nothing was looked on or talked about, or criticised, but the motors. A lesson to the mechanics of this country was taught by the foreigners, smart, alert, quick to obey orders, patient withal. The gentler sex were much in evidence, and in the brilliant sunshine the varied costumes added a wealth of colour to the scene. Several of the continental and trans-Atlantic grand dames, with the latest motoring confections, promenaded round the weighing ring.*

So great was the crowd that Head Constable Salmon and his twenty-five officers had to use ropes to isolate the weighing area. The ceremony was supervised by Naas borough surveyor J.J. Inglis, Lyons Sampson of the Automobile Club and French timekeeper, V. Tampier. Fernand Gabriel led the queue of competing cars, as eleven o'clock chimed from a nearby clock and a French tricolour flew gaily from an adjacent building. His Mors was just within the 1000kg limit and he wheeled it off himself from the scales. This consisted of two L-shaped Stanley machines with a rail across each one, which the cars ascended via a wooden block.

Owen's car was next. A fence-side expert immediately pronounced that the Americans had no chance in the race. 'How could a car have spirit enough to win a race when it found itself picked out with red and green flourishes like a sewing machine?' he queried. A big cheer went up as Selwyn Edge approached with the first of the green Napiers. All went smoothly until the German machines were examined. Suddenly there was drama as officials rejected the Mercedes tyres on the grounds that, though manufactured by Michelin in Germany, they contained fabric of Belgian origin. Also, some valve parts had been imported from France.

Foxhall-Keene agreed to use German-made Continental tyres, but de Caters and Jenatzy, looking like a coalman in his leather jacket and dark clothes, argued for some time before finally bowing to the inevitable. A Michelin representative immediately cabled Germany for valves manufactured there. But a subsequent meeting of the International Commission ratified its decision to exclude the Mercedes drivers should they race with non-German tyres.

*Paris–Bordeaux–Naas. Henry Farman's battle-scarred Panhard.*

His Kildare friends had apparently taught Louis Mooers some Irish tricks. He attempted to ease the officials' task by handing them a piece of paper with his estimate of his car's weight! The Peerless was weighed nevertheless and he was forced to shed the silencer and tool box, and substitute a retaining strap on the battery box to keep within the weight limit. Henry Farman's Panhard was also in trouble: he had to substitute a lighter aluminium water pump for the original brass one.

The excitement mounted when Rene de Knyff's Panhard was found to be as generously overweight as its driver. Despite the misunderstanding about the tyres, the German team representatives had impressed the natives with their stolidity. The French, by contrast, dramatically raised the temperature with eloquent remonstrations and vivid gesticulations. Waving copies of the race regulations written in French, they loudly queried the accuracy of the scales. A delay ensued while fresh weights were obtained from the nearby RIC barracks. As the argument over differing interpretations of 'maximum weight' continued, a spectating farmer suggested they might be better off using the zone system outlined in the new Land Act!

To pacify the French, two of the German cars were rechecked with the new weights. The difference was found to be mere ounces. A British journalist ascribed French surprise at their weight problems to the fact that the Irish system was more accurate than anything they had encountered in previous continental events. De Knyff was forced to jettison various items, including his seat, to make the limit. No sooner were proceedings completed, however, than he furrowed Selwyn Edge's beetle brow even further by smartly replacing it for the race.

Despite the crush, there was only one casualty. Solicitor William Agnew Murphy was lucky not to be impaled when his coat sleeve caught the railings and broke his fifteen-foot fall from the balcony of the nearby Hibernian Bank. As the competing cars were being pushed away, George Prade of *L'Auto* made fun of the ungainly brown leather bag which Jenatzy had mounted on the rear platform as a tool-box. 'Is that for carrying home the Cup?' he rashly disparaged. 'It would fit nicely,' responded an unusually reflective Jenatzy. The Belgian knew something the blinkered Frenchman could not appreciate. That after so many races in 'no-hope' machines, he finally had a car to match those of the competition.

The weighing-in lasted longer than expected and touring cars were substituted for race rehearsals at Kildare. The marshals, timekeepers and their clocks were put through their paces as Waterford's first motorist, Sir William Goff, drove British army Commander-in-Chief, Field Marshal Lord Roberts, around the course. Some competitors later proceeded to Kilcullen where they practised traversing the control areas. Henri Farman stripped a tyre to its cover and J.W. Stocks burst a tyre at Kilcullen Hill, where Mooers incurred the wrath of a local jarvey whom he overtook too closely. Four Napiers provided an exciting race preview as they swept past the Ballyshannon club enclosure. Here, crowds marvelled at the sophisticated telegraph equipment which would flash race news to London, Berlin, Brussels, Paris and New York. Alexander Winton involuntarily added to the Ballshannon excitement, when he hit a pole used in the construction of the stand and damaged his radiator and a wheel.

As well as a large influx of continental correspondents, the UK media gave the race saturation coverage. The *Motor* alone sent 16 journalists. Its *Autocar* rival went one better by bringing a 36-foot diameter hot-air balloon of 21,000 cubic feet. Anchored beside an attendant traction engine just ahead of the Ballyshannon stand, the three-passenger balloon promised spectacular ascents during the race. The device was to be cut free afterwards, to continue its merry advertising way across the plains of Ireland. Bovril announced that it would also fly a balloon over the course. It would release coupons, whose lucky finders would be awarded hampers of Bovril products. Loftily disdaining such gimmickry, Oxo advertised that it was supplying the British team at each control with tins of its 'refreshment without waiting.'

*Jenatzy's pristine car on the scales.*

But not all Kildare people would enjoy the pageantry, or the display of wealth and cutting-edge technology. An army bugler was killed by lightning on the Curragh straight the week before the race. After his horse-drawn trap was seen wandering driverless along the road, Michael Byrne of Caragh was found dead beside a badly-injured companion at the same place. Both had fallen while trying to close the trap's door; drink had been consumed.

'Death due to debility and exposure 'was the inquest verdict on Thomas Byrne of Craddockstown, whose body was discovered in a nearby field. And after the vigilant caretaker of St. Thomas's, Newbridge locked in William Scully and Patrick and Lawrence Kavanagh whom he found sleeping in a college outhouse, local magistrate P.J. Doyle, ensured that they too would not rub shoulders with the Lord Lieutenant's party. He sentenced them to one month each for vagrancy (little room at that Christian institution for a peripatetic carpenter and his pregnant wife, who might have wandered in 1,903 years earlier!)

'Dublin is a petrol-smelling Saturnalia!' wrote *The Field*. Race-fever in the capital exceeded even that at Naas. The city was taken over by fantastically-clad alien automobilists, hotels were filled to the brim. Many English tourists had taken advantage of the fast nine-hour service from London to Dublin. No fewer than four hundred cars came via the regular Holyhead–Dublin route, while other cross-channel motorists came through ports as far south as Waterford. Scottish Automobile Club members commandeered the Gresham Hotel, their airy kilts adding a dash of traditional colour to the display of strange motoring outfits. Business was also said to be booming in the part of the city noted for its nocturnal temptations. A lady visitor did her bit for Women's Liberation by riding a motorcycle — 'the first of her sex seen in Dublin on an automobile-bike.'

Dublin Metropolitan Police officers amiably explained the rules of the road to uncomprehending foreigners. Both the *Irish Cyclist* and police chief Colonel Ross of Bladensburg exhorted drivers and cyclists to comply strictly with traffic regulations, and to co-operate with the police and officials. Irish Automobile Club President Horace Plunkett, however, set an unforgivably bad example when he ignored English regulations in his efforts to reach Ireland for the race! He rashly sped past a car load of police and soldiers in the Welsh town of Bangor. They wired ahead to Holyhead, where he was fined five pounds 'for furious driving.'

The Dublin weather rivalled that of Naas. The sun shone from a cloudless sky. An *Evening Herald* columnist lyricised: 'It was a day on which it felt good to be alive — and to be alive in Ireland!' As the last arrivals hastened in from Kingstown port, Dubliners took to the footpaths in their hundreds to marvel at the strange accents, clothes and machinery. Many visiting cars sported their national colours, the French tricolour, the familiar Union Jack and a spattering of Stars and Stripes. Crowds flocked to admire the Gordon Bennett Cup in West's window at 18/19 College Green. Also displayed were the official badges and armbands, for which Switzers had supplied over 1,000 yards of wide ribbon. Another focal point was the race Information Office in Sackville Street, which was besieged by foreigners.

British MPs, French counts and German barons jostled each other at Huttons of Summerhill (who had once built a state coach for Queen Victoria), as they prepared their cars for the journey to the circuit. 'But for Henley, we'd have a jolly sight more here,' an Englishman insisted, as he fought his way into the Shelbourne Hotel which doubled as the ACGBI headquarters. Constructor Montague Napier raised a cheer on Sackville Street, as he sped off with his car's silencer removed. Diversifying street vendors did a roaring trade in both fruit and race programmes. One knowledgeable shawlie was heard educating an ignorant onlooker on the role of the chauffeur. 'He's the shuvver, sir. You put him behind the car and he shoves it up the hills!'

Long before the arrival of the automobile and the Gordon Bennett racers, the Dublin jarveys were the daredevil drivers of their day. A columnist paid

*The centuries collide at Naas weigh-in.*

tribute to their speed and skill; 'Your driver will take all the chances that a crowded thoroughfare gives him; he would scorn to leave more than an inch between your foot and a Guinness beer dray; he will shake your flounces and furebelows in the very windows of the passing trams, but he is beloved by the gods and nothing ever happens to him.'

Some of the more enterprising Gordon Bennett visitors forsook their machines to sample the jarvies' expertise on a sidecar city tour. The *Freeman's Journal* reported 'It was one of the humours of the day to see parties of foreigners abandon their twentieth century chariots and, still clad in their leathers and macintoshes, submit to being driven about by the dashing nags.' Following a rewarding tour of the city's Georgian quarter, however, an English duo soon found that the gods were on a break. They were pitched out after a head-on collision between their sidecar and another near the river. 'And they said the automobile is dangerous,' one was heard to remark, as he retrieved his bowler. They were luckier than the unfortunate furniture van driver who was killed when his horse ran amuck in Cork that afternoon.

Apart from the speed thrills, visitors were richly rewarded by the jarveys' ready wit. A Old Harrovian pedant got his comeuppance in the Phoenix Park. When he informed his older jarvey that there was no such bird as a phoenix, the man promptly rejoined 'An' shure, yer honour, neither is there any such park as this!' As a party of fastidious Americans clip-clopped across the Liffey after viewing Gandon's domed Four Courts, they remarked on the obvious health hazard of the odiferous low-tide waters. 'Typhoid, is it?' the jarvey exclaimed rhetorically. 'Sure no typhoid germ that was ever hatched could live in it for an hour!'

Nearer the circuit and conscious of its place as the focus of international attention, the prescient *Leinster Leader* waxed eloquent in a leader of which Fleet Street should have been envious.

*Now, however, on the eve of the struggle, whose outcome will be 'local news' for the globe at large, the association of the steam-roller, the stand-builder, and the speculators keenly 'on the make' cannot check the reflective mind in its estimate of the magnificence of next Thursday's happening. The Motor-Derby, no matter how much one may decry it as an advertising medium for Automobilism, nevertheless marks a notable stage in the progress of human invention and practical science. As such, it confers a certain world-wide distinction on its chosen area. The roads over which the flying motors will skim will be coupled in history with the most strenuous efforts of Man to achieve the 'last conquest' of Distance and to add the final triumph to the victories of territorial locomotion.*

On the day on which future flier Amy Johnson was born, the *Leader* continued:

*Next to aerial navigation, the motor car represents the highest attainable possibilities in the way of human travelling. A vehicle, flashing by at the rate of 80 to 100 miles an hour is an experience which the average mind can with difficulty even imagine. From the standpoint of a century ago, it is a miracle. Yet to the Automobilists of today it is but an accomplished fact, thresholding other and perhaps more wonderful things. The day when the man of business and leisure will career along the highways and bye-ways at Express Speed may be of course far distant — but who — with the reaped harvests of science and invention before him — can doubt that some similar revolution will in future generations relegate the train, the tram and the cycle to the same category as the Stage Coach. Automoblism therefore, as it is expanded on Thursday, has the intense interest and fascination that attaches to everything which makes world history, and that heralds a greater human empire over space and time. To this aspect of the Gordon Bennett contest, even the most sordid mind — and the more utterly callous to the other elements of personal risk and peril — cannot be insensible.*

The *Leader* concluded:

*The Motor Race is truly 'Great', not as the enterprise of Trade or the fad of Wealth, not as the occasion of a great International gathering, not as an opportunity of persons as profit or pleasure bent. It derives its importance and grandeur from its demonstration of Twentieth Century mechanical skill and its prophecy of the travelling future. The localities where opportunity has made this possible must derive permanent note from their connection with this latest test of human and mechanical endurance — and this circumstance can not be unwelcome in a country where everything that lends distinction and individuality to a district is highly valued.*

Gordon Bennett excitement was as intense in Athy as in Dublin. In addition to the foreign accents, locals were treated to the strange patois of policemen who had been drafted in from as far away as Galway, Limerick and Cork. Townspeople welcomed the influx of automobiles and business — particularly as motorists drove so considerately following adverse publicity when an errant driver had frightened a local priest's horse. Too slowly, in fact. One native complained to a councillor that his ass and cart had been held up by a car in front!

Even the Barrow basked in the excitement. It hosted many flag-bedecked houseboats, including one rented by Harvey du Cros who endeavoured to keep everyone happy by flying a Union Jack on a rich emerald background. The presence of the German team was a major attraction in the town. Camille Jenatzy had become a favourite of the postmistress, as he called each day to send postcards of local views to his daughters in Belgium. An American visitor was disappointed, however, when he asked a bartender for something on the rocks. 'You are a joker!' the latter replied 'Where in the name of Jaysus would you get ice in the middle of summer?'

The *Kildare Observer* noted:

*Over all, could be heard the polyglot babble of the polished French, the inharmonious but vigorously guttural of the Germans — all commingling with the nasal twang of the Yankees and the peculiar idiom of the Londoners. In truth, the inhabitants of Athy have had a novel and unique experience, with motor vehicles from colossal carriages to the daintiest armchair. Magnificent saloons, canopied and upholstered in the most extravagant manner, and huge omnibuses large enough to accommodate the inhabitants of some ark, not to speak of myriads of motor-racers, roadsters and hacks, all careering through the streets.*

With understandably little knowledge of either drivers or cars, some media canvassed drivers rather than offer their own opinion on the likely racewinner. With the first five Paris–Madrid finishers in the country, as well as the Gordon Bennett contestants, they were spoiled for choice. Baron de Caters predicted a German success, while Louis Mooers suggested the English because of their circuit knowledge. The experienced Jarrott regarded Henri Farman as favourite, while Camille Jenatzy and Jean Salleron supported Fernand Gabriel. Selwyn Edge acknowledged that the French had three of the finest drivers in the world, but he confined himself to forecasting that the winner would average 45 mph. He left no doubt as to the importance of success 'which would bring millions of pounds to the country of the winning car and work for thousands of mechanics.'

The *Daily Express* picked 'the young, brave and lucky' Gabriel as race favourite, with Jarrott a close second. The *Irish Independent* concurred, though it had some concern that this was the first time the French had driven on the left side of the road! The paper also dismissed de Knyff as being too old and Jenatzy as an unlucky daredevil. With typical Celtic abandon, it projected the Americans as the dark horses of the event. No one selected Camille Jenatzy, of whom the widespread impression — as enduring as Van Goth's bandaged ear — was that of a driver standing forlornly trackside with either a broken machine or a bloodied body. Despite his ground-breaking mile a minute, the wild Belgian was seen as a permanently earth-anchored Across. None gave him a chance against his Mors or Panhard rivals, particularly the polished and calmer veteran, Rene de Knyff.

The *Irish Independent* was on surer ground with the weather. 'Bring a luncheon basket, field glasses, a programme and waterproof wraps — and make an early start,' it advised. Other Dublin newspapers printed maps of the course, and helpful advice on the most suitable and accessible vantage points. Hely's of Dame Street published a state-of-the art Guide to the Irish Fortnight, priced sixpence, and a selection of thirteen Gordon Bennett picture postcards for a penny each. Last minute fears of a petrol famine were relieved when the Anglo-American Oil Company not only guaranteed adequate supplies, but also reduced the price from two shillings and sixpence per gallon to one shilling and eightpence. An enterprising Dubliner claimed to have discovered oil in a cellar well. The *Car Illustrated* reported that it was 'very dilute!'

Hordes of race-goers assembled at the Moat of Ardcsull on the evening before the race. Their numbers rivalled the myriad bluebells and violets which had hitherto sheltered undisturbed under the tall trees. As if accompanying a Crusade or some medieval expedition, a variety of private tents sprouted over-night like the local mushrooms. All forty-two members of the Yorkshire Automobile Club established their own colourful encampment. 'Moat' was described as a rather cheerful misnomer by a Cockney, as he fixed his candle in the neck of any empty Bass bottle; 'Not much of a moated granse. It must be the contrariness of the

*Tents sprouted overnight at the Moat of Ardscull.*

country that makes them call this hillock a moat, just as they call a fence a ditch!'

Some queried the wisdom of paying so much to sleep on a bag of straw — which they had to fill themselves. Others did not sleep at all, as tipsy revellers regressed to Boy Scout youth and sang around the many fires until the small hours. 'I never again want to hear "Dolly Gray" or "My Dear Little Shamrock",' one exhausted camper protested later. Members of the Press were also unamused, when disrespectful youths collapsed their tent and exposed their frailty to the moonlight.

But for the competitors, it was a time for reflection. Selwyn Edge remembered that the eve of the race provided:

> ... *one of the glorious evenings which stand out in one's memory. It had been a hot day and the peacefulness of the countryside was in sharp contrast to the turmoil which would be raging within a few short hours. At one moment, nature in all her loveliness, unstained by the hand of man, was on all sides, but by daybreak all this would be forgotten and the thoughts of every man and woman on this island would be centred on a speed contest when the lives of many would be suspended by a hair. One error of judgement, one false turn of a wheel or the pressure of a lever a second too late and nothing but disaster could fall.*

The Napier driver's feelings were no doubt heightened by the awareness that as winner last year he would be the first to start. But his team-mate Jarrott was even more disturbed by grim forebodings, as he observed that same striking Turner sunset.

> *It was solemn and impressive, and as I stood there and watched it, a strange feeling of impending disaster seemed to come over me. Never before or since then, before the start of a race, have I ever felt it was possible that under any circumstances I could come to grief, and yet that night I felt that some great catastrophe was in store for me. I do not know why I had this feeling, but the more I tried to shake it off, the more depressed I became.*
>
> *With the bustle and confusion, noise and animation around me, it seems strange that I should have had this idea of the possibility of everything not going right. Although I had not expressed the opinion to a soul, I had nevertheless in my own mind felt that no one had a better chance of winning on the following day as myself. I went to bed very early, having previously for some cause I could not understand, sealed up all my personal papers and addressed them to the persons interested, also leaving a note of general instructions in case of anything happening on the following day.*

# 10 Start Your Engines!

Packed trains — birds take flight — 'Mephistophelian' Jenatzy's fiery start — Winton stranded

The race start was scheduled for seven in the morning. Like a flock of starlings, one hundred members of the North Dublin Cycling Club descended on the General Post office just after midnight. With the cool east wind behind them, they set out along the quays with tinkling bells and laden carriers for distant Kildare.

While competitors enjoyed their last few hours of rest, race-day had already commenced for many Dubliners. The city arose to the sound of starting engines and the rattling of door knockers, as the less affluent woke their neighbours and hastened to the trains at Kingsbridge railway station. According to the *Evening Herald*, 'the hotels were as animated as daytime, even though dark. Indeed, the city seemed not to have slept; cycle shops and motor shops were all centres of bustling activity.'

Even at four in the morning, spectators lined Cork Hill and Dame Street to cheer departing motorists. 'As daybreak drew near, nothing was heard but the whirring of motor machinery and the tooting of horns,' wrote the *Evening Mail*. Dublin Corporation entered into the spirit of the occasion with its customary famed aplomb. An Inchicore road-mending programme reduced the width of the main exit by two thirds and caused the city's first recorded automobile traffic jam.

The *Evening Herald* greeted the historic day with an enthusiastic and optimistic leader:

> *Ireland is fortunate in having been set as the scene of this great drama of speed and daring, for not alone is the spectacle itself one of tremendous interest, but the pecuniary profit which it incidentally confers is very considerable. Apart from these immediate advantages, the Irish public have good reason to look with a friendly eye upon the advance of the motor. It is likely before long to effect a revolution in locomotion, and it may ultimately help to solve the Irish industrial problem.*

As the last of the cars departed in the pink-tinted dawn, the jarveys regained possession of the streets. They did a roaring trade to the trains which were advertised to depart 'when full.' This was loosely interpreted. Even the race officials' specially booked carriage was crammed to Indian-train proportions by determined race-goers, an unprecedented percentage of whom were female. Over 500 cyclists added bruised shins, colourful language and further logistical problems, as they pressed aboard with their trusty steeds.

The crowds were good news for the programme sellers. At least one programme was put to extracurricular use by a local Fagin, whom a DMP officer observed using it as a cover for picking pockets! Trains staggered to their destinations on time despite the chaos, though Athy officials had to sprint to reach their positions by the appointed five thirty deadline. Passengers immediately set out on foot from Athy, Kildare, Newbridge and Maryboro stations for the best vantage points. A party of 50 Mancunians stimulated their early morning pace with a walking race. A two guineas-prize greeted the first to reach the Moat of Ardscull.

Apart from the crowds who left by train, thousands more travelled by foot and on bicycle, many carrying baskets of provisions. The road from Dublin to Naas was covered by a solid cloud of dust raised by the cars. But, despite the traffic, not one serious accident was reported. Pedestrians and motorists alike were greeted royally by early-rising villagers, who gazed eagerly over their half-doors at the unlikely dusty throng which came with the brightening dawn. *Autocar* wrote: 'It was the greatest wonder that the drivers in the dark had no tumble, for on one footpath there would be two or three cyclists with lights on and on the opposite two or three more without lamps, and to complicate matters, jaunting cars would be proceeding along in a string of three or four straggling all over the road. This was the case all the way to Naas.'

Some budgets took a modest tumble, however, as jarveys requested five shillings a head to transport passengers from Athy to the Moat of Ardscull. 'You wouldn't grudge it; it does not come every day!', one driver beguiled the *Belfast Telegraph* reporter. As Club Enclosure race-goers queued to wash and brush the dust off their clothes, a water shortage brought an unexpected bonus for equally sharp local farmers who charged a shilling a bucket.

Spectators who arrived early saw the circuit at its greenest and most beautiful. Blue wreaths of smoke curled upwards from many fires at the Moat of Ardscull. Glinting off the yellow-tinted *Autocar* balloon, early sunshine enlivened the dewdrops and brought the whitethorn hedges to sweet-smelling life. As joyous birdsong completed the Arcadian tableau, a more unlikely site could hardly be imagined for the forthcoming contest between the fleetest and most powerful products of cutting-edge automobile technology. But before the last mists had ungirdled themselves from the Dunamase hills, the peace was rudely disturbed by the noise of arriving cars and the exciting sight of Edge, Stocks, Winton and Owen heading for the startline.

Vans and supply machines had earlier deposited tyres, oil, and tools at pre-selected points around the circuit. Athy and the main control areas were enlivened by the tents of the Continental Tyre Company and Dunlop, whose representatives distributed no fewer than 150 tyres. Supplies of Pratt's Motor Spirit and the Vacuum Oil Company were laid out beside the Napier service station. Large tubs of water stretched along a bank of broken stones ready to cool tyres and fill thirsty radiators. Beside the petrol cans and buckets, an army of men took temporary rest on wooden packing cases. The French sported traditional blue overalls, while the English wore green ties to match the Napier colours. The team personnel would hand drivers whatever they needed, but only the driver and his mechanic were allowed to work on each car.

Staff at all the control points were assembled for action. Spectators provided appropriate encouragement for train-delayed Athy officials who hurriedly marked out the control lines with whitewash. The timekeepers composed themselves for their 14-hour day around a table borrowed from a nearby thatched cottage. A large basket of bottled nourishment arrived. 'Yous can start now all right!' an envious wag shouted.

The start area presented the most animated and colourful spectacle. Bright bunting and the flags of the competing countries flew gaily from the official grandstand just after the startline. This was marked by a modest roadside post close to Tippeenan Lane and a flag on the opposite banking. An unlikely, but soon to be historic, Gate of Hercules.

*Heading for the start. Baron de Caters whose wife didn't want him to race.*

Nearby were the large marquees of the caterers and telegraph operators. Hundreds of train spectators streamed by with their baskets and bottles. Drafts of RIC men marched off to allocated patrol points, grub-bags swinging against their hips. Fruit vendors' exhortations mixed with the excited buzz of the walkers and cyclists. Picknickers used fallen tree trunks for tables, and the appetising aroma of frying bacon permeated the merry Breugel scene. Photographers roamed the area or took short cuts across the clover-reeking fields, cinematograph operators reinforced their strategic corner positions. Good humour bridged the gap between the busy RIC officers and disorientated foreign visitors.

At six a.m. precisely, race officials and the RIC under the control of Colonel Neville Chamberlain, swung into action. The roads were closed. Every cross-roads, laneway and junction was blocked off and, as motorists had already noticed, not an animal or fowl was to be seen anywhere around the circuit. The preparations were paying off. This was to be no Paris–Madrid — the Irish would show the foreigners a thing or two!

Even the local postmistress had to walk through the fields to deliver her mail. 'But I am His Majesty the King's post-office representative,' she plaintively protested, as clouds jostled ominously in the distance and threw the Ardscull camp into sharp relief. Parts of the Curragh were exclusively under military control. Across country from Ballyshannon, the crisp note of a bugle shattered the morning air to denote that His Majesty's subjects would no longer be free to use the King's highway. The din of the vendors and the importunities of 'the Ring' amused the French and Germans. 'Five to one, Jarrott. Six to one de Knyff!' they shouted. One brave Frenchman dismayed his compatriots by backing Jarrott, whom he described as the best driver in the race.

At six thirty, the pilot cars driven by Joseph Lisle and Lieutenant Mansfield Smith-Cumming set off to patrol the course prior to the contest. As they slithered away, it was evident that the start area had been too liberally coated with dust retardant. In their haste to complete the previous night's laying, the whiskey-fuelled workers had poured the last can on the road undiluted, instead of mixing it in the correct proportions of one part of Westrumite to nineteen of water. Dilution was perhaps an alien concept for Irish whiskey connoisseurs! Fresh sand was quickly laid to mitigate the ice-rink effect.

The patrol presented the only other faux pas of the day. Instead of the cars separately covering the east and west circuits, Lisle followed his companion westwards and then compounded the confusion by breaking down. This meant that the Kilcullen to Carlow stretch was not patrolled at all. The carefully planned organisation proved equal to the challenge, however. The RIC and race officials ensuring a watertight road closure.

The racing cars noisily approached the marshalling area. There was a cool breeze and subdued sunshine as the minutes ticked away. The powerful machines looked surreally out of place in such a peaceful setting. Louis Mooers had been the first to arrive. 'Just as happy as ever!' he replied to a journalist who asked him how he felt. Fernand Gabriel next parked his Paris–Madrid winning machine beside Johnny Rubon's cottage, whose railings were newly painted for the big occasion.

Foxhall-Keene arrived in his Mercedes. The 33-year old American spoke to his wife for a while, before sitting quietly and alone on a grassy bank to await the start. He may well have reflected that many of the Paris–Madrid drivers had witnessed such a scene, before they sped to their deaths. Like the poor, the rich playboys were also victims of circumstance, but their contribution to motoring was not be derided. Foxhall-Keene had demonstrated skill and staying power in the Paris–Vienna marathon; affluent amateurs like he and Baron de Caters were among the bravest and ablest of the pioneers.

*Foxhall-Keene and mechanic, Willy Luttgen, ready themselves for the 327-mile marathon.*

The continentals were surrounded by animated and vociferous compatriots. Mechanics raced hither and thither, speaking excitedly in French and German, or with American and English accents. There seemed to be as many officials as racers on the line. His rusty beard matching his tweed jacket and cap, the stocky starter Colonel Lindsay Lloyd and France's V. Tampier explained the starting method to drivers for the last time. Acting as interpreter, Justice of the Peace Henry Norman translated for Gabriel and Jenatzy, the only non English-speaking drivers in the race. The buzz of expectant spectators filled the pre-storm quiet. And, then, the moment for which everyone had been waiting. The birds took flight. The ground shook. Conversation ceased. Eyes and hearts focused on its high-mounted driver, as the first engine roared into impatient life at three minutes before seven.

As winner of the 1902 Cup, Selwyn Edge in his number-one car had the honour of leading off the race at seven o'clock. A pistol shot was to be his starting signal. He would be followed at seven minute intervals by each of the other eleven drivers, who would receive a verbal countdown and command. Clad in a long white coat and with a set and determined face, the 35-year old English team leader confidently placed his green Napier on the startline. He was greeted by welcoming cheers, as Dunlop technicians pumped the last puffs of air into the tyres. He noted the contrast between this organised scene and those continental races with their uncontrolled and unpredictable onlookers. Racing in Ireland was certainly going to be less worrisome, particularly on roads with which he had become so familiar, if only at touring speed.

'I'd had a good sleep and I felt extraordinarily fit,' he subsequently recalled. 'There was a very large gathering of friends on the line and after Cecil and I had taken our places in the car, a dozen hands reached out to wish us God Speed. The fateful moment approached. The starter, watch in hand, took up his position on the line; the engine was started up, and then came the warnings "Two minutes, one minute, twenty seconds, ten seconds"....'

At five seconds to go, Edge clicked the lever into its first-gear notch. Lindsay Lloyd fired his starting pistol and stood back. A great shout, a mighty intimation of power, and the green Napier blasted away. Edge bent his head down, as if to acknowledge the encouraging cheers. He accelerated rapidly under the grandstand until, clear of the oiled portion of the circuit, his car disappeared over the brow of the rising ground in a great cloud of dust. The *Autocar* correspondent wrote 'As it took the open road beyond, it was shut out by the white wall of its own raising and the first hope of England was gone.'

The crowd buzzed with amazement at Edge's speed. The waiting tension had been broken. Their anticipation grew as they eagerly awaited the next starter, Rene de Knyff. Clad in a bulging belted macintosh, and wearing his trademark yachtsman's peaked cap, the 39-year old veteran of so many classic races approached. This was an important event for the French team leader, whose early reign as the world's best was now under threat from younger drivers.

De Knyff's burly presence was matched only by that of the banker, Baron de Rothschild, who greeted him on the line. High in his dark blue car, de Knyff smiled broadly and acknowledged the enthusiastic reception of a virtual guard of honour of compatriots with wildly waving straw hats. He clipped on his goggles. A journalist noted 'As he sat imperturbably behind his steering wheel, his massive figure seemed the embodiment of calm courage, combined with the qualities of resourcefulness, dash and unlimited staying power.' Not as quick to accelerate as Edge, the Panhard driver took both hands off the wheel to wave to spectators as he sped away to a chorus of repeated cries of 'Vive la France!'

*The three faces of Camille Jenatzy ...*

*... 7.15 a.m: Amiable greetings for startline friends ...*

*... 7.18 a.m: Jenatzy the racer lowers the shutters on the outside world ...*

*... 7.21 a.m: The focused Red Devil takes over!*

Percy Owen next brought his Winton to the line at 7.14. The 28-year old was warmly applauded by a large party of compatriots, as he led the first American motor racing team into European battle. His car looked flimsy compared with the first two starters. As Owen sat upright in his black macintosh and brown cap, observers noted that it seemed to offer the least shelter from the full force of the wind. The pressure of photographers was now making itself felt, officials having to warn them not to obstruct competitors. The sportsmanlike Jarrott who knew what it was like to race on foreign soil bade Owen 'God Speed'. Seconds later the young Cleveland driver released the handbrake and lumbered off, understandably the slowest starter so far in his single-geared machine. Mechanically-minded spectators shuddered as they pondered how that one gear would cope equally with the long straights and the Windy Gap ascent.

The American association continued with the next starter, Camille Jenatzy, whom German officials and spectators greeted rapturously. He drove the off-white number-four Mercedes lent to the German team by the New York millionaire, Clarence Gray Dinsmore. But there was nothing lumbering about the driver, the Red Devil himself. The complete antithesis of de Knyff, Jenatzy's excitement and energy were palpable as he exchanged a final hearty handshake with his friend, Baron de Caters. Clad in a black India-rubber smock strapped around his waist and a sailor's Sou' Western hat, the 35-year old Belgian restlessly awaited the starter's orders. His demeanour attracted the journalists, one of whom wrote 'His smile or frown tells very little; you know he has bigger thoughts than anything facial can delineate.' *Car Illustrated* described him as 'A man of obviously high-strung temperament, with sandy hair and a Mephistophelian beard. His presence suggested the recrudescence of an extinct volcano.'

Jenatzy's take-off was appropriately volcanic. Great sheets of flame belched from the Mercedes. Its wheels revolved dramatically, tearing grooves in the road as he made what *Autocar* described as the best start of the day. He glanced down momentarily at the offside spinning wheel, touched his hat briefly in appreciation of the applause and disappeared rapidly over the horizon.

Wearing white shoes, white coat and green cap, Charles Jarrott was the fifth starter in his green Napier. As he went to the line, he suddenly realised that for the first time, he was starting a race on home English-speaking territory. A popular figure, Jarrott was greeted on the line by as many continental as British and Irish friends. Six feet tall, he towered over his 17-year old mechanic, Cecil Bianchi, the youngest race participant. As the 26-year old Napier driver calmly smoked a cigarette and gathered his concentration, an observer described him as 'looking as keen and unconcerned as if off on a run to Brighton.'

Jarrott's calm, however, was disturbed by the sudden cracking sound of breaking branches, as an overladen tree deposited its intrepid human cargo on the nearby road. The Englishman glanced momentarily to his right before returning his concentration to the track ahead. His clipboard under his left arm, Lindsay Lloyd counted down the final seconds. Then, with a great roar from the engine, the Napier raced quickly away. As they sped into the dust and the cries of 'Good luck, Jarrott!' faded behind them, Bianchi expectantly settled himself low behind the scuttle. He was happy with their car. Like his driver, he had every reason to be confident of a good result on the circuit they had got to know so well over the preceding weeks.

Fernand Gabriel was next off at 7.35. However, he had to briefly share the limelight and the road with another vehicle, a small cart which had been commandeered to remove the broken branches. Before the race, *The Automotor Journal* had glibly remarked 'Of course, a donkey in the land of dreams, and in the middle of the road, would be an unpleasant object to encounter at the speed of the Gordon Bennett race!' But, now, it was the humble donkey which had come to the rescue of the automobilists. A more incongruous scene could hardly be imagined, as the animal twitched its ears beside the mighty smoking machine which had just averaged over 65 mph in the Paris–Madrid race. 'It's the thirteenth competitor!' some onlookers joked.

*Charles Jarrott — 'as unconcerned as if off on a run to Brighton.'*

The sky was cloudy and overcast, as the 23-year old Breton awaited his orders, surrounded by voluble compatriots. Tyre-manufacturer Andre Michelin was among those who wished him luck. A win by Gabriel would restore the lustre and the loot Michelin lost to Dunlop after Selwyn Edge's 1902 success. A reporter noted that, as Gabriel sat low in the streamlined Mors, 'It seemed more racer than any other machine — it had beauty and speed in its lines.' And speed the machine immediately displayed as, enveloped by a huge exhaust halo, it leaped eagerly away into the opening circuit. Gabriel was understandably confident of success, following the car's superb Paris–Madrid performance.

Sporting dark goggles, a check cap back to front and with an American flag pinned over his heart, Mooers was next to start. 'It's a flying meat safe' laughed one spectator, as the Peerless lined up with its long see-through gauze bonnet. A turn of the starting handle tested the ignition but anxiety quickly clouded the American's youthful face, as the engine suddenly

*Fernand Gabriel and his Mors — 'beauty and speed in its lines.'*

spluttered and stopped. His mechanic then push-started the car and a precocious fruit vendor shouted 'Mister, you left your handbrake on!' As the engine fired up and the brake was released, mechanic W.H. Starin leaped back on board the slowly-moving machine. Despite his hesitant start, due possibly to an excessively high low gear, Mooers was accompanied on his way by loud hurrahs, thanks no doubt to that earlier Green dalliance.

Female hearts fluttered at the sight of the finely-cut aristocratic features of Baron de Caters, as he prepared to leave with his mechanic, Gustave Girard, at eleven minutes before eight. The debonair Baron had a lot riding on this race. He had played a key role in not only assuring Mercedes that the 60 hp cars were fast and reliable enough to win the race, but also in insisting that Camille Jenatzy be allowed a drive. After final adjustments and a last look around the car, the smiling Belgian secured his cap back to front and clipped on his goggles. As the seconds ticked away, Grey Dinsmore wished him and his mechanic good luck. The 28-year old Baron's reputation for eagle-eyed alertness proved well-founded. He rocketed away at a great rate — but between changing from first to second gears, he found time to blow a kiss to his wife who had not wanted him to race She was to watch anxiously all day from her seat in the centre of the front row in the Grandstand. It would take a long time to lay the ghosts of Paris–Madrid.

*Hesitant start for Louis Mooers.*

As eight o'clock approached, England's last representative came to the line. Resplendant in another long white coat and green cap, 33-year old J.W. Stocks was no stranger to Irish roads. But this was his first motor race apart from the pre-race English Trials, and he made an understandably nervous start. Nevertheless, he looked as determined as Selwyn Edge as he likewise rapidly gained speed. The Napier bounded along the ground before disappearing into the dust, which was now abating thanks to the passage of the earlier starters.

A tangible link with the last of the great city-to-city races was provided by the next starter, Henry Farman in his louvre-bonneted Panhard. Still clearly visible on its radiator was the 51 number which he had so recently carried from Paris to Bordeaux. Having competed in the Circuit des Ardennes race, the Athy course held no terrors for the Panhard exponent who must have felt he could adapt better to its convolutions than his older team-mate, de Knyff. Today might well be the day the 29-year old would depose the veteran.

Looking more Mexican than European, the happy moustachioed driver was swamped by French supporters as he came to the line. They quickly scattered, however, as the impatient engine burst into life with a volley of explosions. It as suddenly faltered and stopped. Ten seconds were lost before a quick turn of the starting handle brought it back to life again, to launch Farman into the distance ere the cheering of his supporters had died away.

'He should have stuck to the gigis,' a fence-side player unkindly observed as the intrepid steeplechaser James Foxhall-Keene let in the clutch too quickly. With insufficient revs, the unusually reflective Foxie ingloriously stalled the engine of his Mercedes. He then left the ignition fully advanced. His mechanic, Willy Luttgen, would have been knocked down by turning the handle, had the error not been noticed in time. The 33-year old Irish-American's 8.17 getaway was one of the most hesitant of the morning. But he was soon to redeem himself with some swift and capable lappery.

The unluckiest driver was the last starter, Alexander Winton, whose wife and 14-year old son had travelled from America to see him race. Earlier in the morning, Henry Ford's 43-year old friend had hit a stone wall on a sharp corner in Athy — his second contretemps in two days. And as if to confirm the chalked Club enclosure anagram 'Win not', his car now refused to start due to fuel-feed problems. Lindsay Lloyd gave him the official word to start, before Winton and his mechanic, Armstrong, set about stripping the carburettor system. A marshal suggested they move from the course to a side road. 'I am still in the race, on the course and doing time,' the American responded to loud applause.

He placed his car as close to the bank as possible. As time ticked away, it quickly became evident that the early starters would arrive before the hapless American had even commenced racing. The Winton's raised and well-polished bonnet mirrored the car's number and the two men, as they patiently toiled under the encouraging but inhibiting eyes of onlookers. But spectators' ears were soon focused southwards for the first sound of the approaching Selwyn Edge.

*Cup defender Selwyn Edge was to enjoy a meteoric opening lap.*

# 1.1 Eventful First Lap

Spectators aghast at Edge's speed — Foxhall-Keene's surprise —
Stocks loops the loop — de Knyff survives —
Jenatzy and Owen confrontation

After racing up the slope from Ballyshannon to Kilcullen, Selwyn Edge safely negotiated the acute right hairpin turn which directed him to the fast run southwards. His progress was as meteoric as his start, and he reached Castledermot and Carlow long before expected. He wrote subsequently:

*'I have a unique recollection of a mighty cheer going up on the part of our well-wishers, as the clutch was let in and the gears changed to cover that initial stretch to the fork we had to take to the southern loop. Great gods, how that car did go! I had let her out more than once during practice, but on this occasion she seemed to know what was expected of her.*

Those pre-race reconnaissance laps proved their worth, as the Napier driver raced ahead faultlessly. Rene de Knyff, however, soon shed some of his legendary calm and precious minutes. Missing the fast deceptive left curve, he went straight up the inviting Oak Park escape road at Ballymoon corner near Gurteen bridge. The 'Y' junction where the old Mail road divided between Castledermot and Carlow proved to be the biggest hazard of the opening lap — locals felt that its danger should have been more clearly advertised to competitors. Ironically, it was the stretch on which Carlow Council had expended particular effort, improving and steamrolling the previously badly-drained surface.

*'They'll be here any minute!' Waiting in style for the racers.*

De Knyff uprooted the wire fencing and was lucky to escape without damage. Spectators marvelled at his speed and coolness as he quickly reversed, pointed the Panhard in the right direction and gathered momentum again. But the incident was not something to settle a driver on his opening lap and it cost him a minimum of two valuable minutes.

Officials were preparing to renew the fence when, less than 15 minutes later, Jenatzy also arrived much too quickly to take the bend. There was no indecision by the Belgian. He likewise opted for the escape road and scattered the workers. But he had braked earlier than his French rival and lost less time. He smartly extricated himself and resumed at unabated pace. De Knyff had another distracting moment entering Castledermot, he braked at an indistinct white line which preceded the correct control entry line. The next arrival, Percy Owen, experienced the same problem. Henry Farman in his haste stopped for neither line and lost precious seconds as he reversed back into the control.

As he passed the opening controls, it was evident that Edge was faster than most of his rivals. He was encouraged by the waves of the hundreds of young and old who thronged the hedges outside Castledermot and Carlow. He had become familiar to them over the previous weeks' practising. Accelerating out of Carlow, the Napier's performance seemed to underline the wisdom of changing to the more powerful car. The Englishman had high hopes of keeping the Gordon Bennett Cup. The town whose roads had been well watered that morning witnessed further fireworks a few minutes later. Percy Owen arrived with Jenatzy hot on his heels. In his excitement, the fast-moving Belgian overshot the control line and then reversed rapidly. 'Here's the devil who will win!' a spectator shouted prophetically.

The Red Devil was in turn closely followed by Jarrott. The English driver later recalled:

> *Jenatzy's frantic excitement when I caught him in Carlow on the first round, after starting seven minutes behind him, I shall never forget. We were delayed there some few minutes under the regulations, and Jenatzy came over to me trembling with rage, because he said, Owen, of the American team just in front, was impeding him. I endeavoured to encourage him, but he got into his car waving his arms and vowing that if the American did not get out of his way there would be bloodshed!*

Another American in the news was Foxhall-Keene who provided the large Carlow crowd with some amusement. The *Motor* correspondent wrote: 'It was distinctly comical to see him, in his dust-covered suiting, grovelling beneath the car, his brake gear having become a little deranged.' 'Foxie' was, however, soon to reiterate that those who provide comedy are invariably very serious persons.

Edge, meantime, continued his circuit-opening lap at unabated pace. Athy boasted the biggest English contingent. A ripple of excitement ran through the town as he arrived at the East Control at six minutes to eight. Officials and spectators at the distant exit control heard the cheering. They didn't believe that the Napier driver had arrived so quickly until the pilot cyclist led him over the crown of the railway bridge. His early arrival worried race officials that he might overrun the later starters at Ballyshannon, only a few miles away. They decided to hold him for twenty one minutes, rather than the planned twelve. After swallowing a sponge cake and some strawberries, Edge impatiently raced off to Ballyshannon and the completion of a flawless opening lap.

*About to outfox the professionals, Foxhall-Keene at Athy.*

Featuring on both the western and eastern circuits, Athy was the most race-conscious town on the course. All the shops were closed and the streets were crowded for the event. Ancient White's Castle had never witnessed such frantic activity, as cars noisily arrived and departed continuously. No sooner had de Knyff followed Edge away than Owen arrived with Jenatzy again snapping at his wheels. A pilot cyclist jumped on his bicycle and escorted the American away almost at competition speed, as the Belgian entered the control.

Jenatzy was held for an extra two minutes in order to restore a safe gap between the two cars. Unlike the urbane de Knyff who found time to shake hands with his head mechanic, the focused Mercedes driver looked straight ahead while speaking to his helpers. Then he sped away, both hands off the steering wheel, while still talking to them! Some officials felt that the faster Jenatzy should have been let restart ahead of Owen, but the pair were allowed to continue in their original order. The immediate arrival of Jarrott at 8.30 soon put the matter out of officials' minds — and before he left, Gabriel arrived! A race steward insisted 'I have never seen such excitement. From eight until 8.50, six of the cars had arrived or been despatched, and during this time, there was not a moment when one or more was not standing on the road near us.'

One of the last arrivals was Louis Mooers. An observer reported that the Peerless 'was without exhaust box and its rattle was ear-splitting.' The car refused to restart for over an hour. But he was more fortunate than the flying Stocks, whose race progress was permanently arrested by that wire fence at Ballymoon's *Lorelei*. The occupants of Henry Bruen's strategic stand again got their money's worth, when the Englishman arrived far too quickly to take the left curve. The fence, sadly, had been very professionally re-erected and one of the poles anchored his front wheel with equal efficiency. It swung the car around and sent the shocked driver somersaulting skywards like those Whirlwind Cyclists of the Tivoli Theatre. Well used to such mishaps from his two-wheeled days, Stocks and his mechanic, Arthur MacDonald were lucky to escape with only bruising. But like the driver's white coat, the British challenge had shed its promising lustre and had been reduced by a third before the completion of even one lap.

The incident underlined the contrast between the perspective of driver and spectator. To onlookers, it seemed a driving error. Some insisted that Stocks should have known the road after all his pre-race practice. The reality for the driver, however, was much different. He explained afterwards:

> *I was doing between 70 and 80 mph when I struck a projection on the road, at the same time as I should be applying my brakes. This displaced me in my seat and momentarily delayed my braking. Seeing the absolutely straight road ahead, I decided to take it and then to reverse out. When I was about three yards away I suddenly saw the wire, but then it was impossible to stop.*

*'Now, you see him…' Stocks speeds towards the high wire.*

*The wire stretched and tore out a supporting pole. My nearside front wheel was held by the pole, and the offside front wheel also broke as the car was swung violently into the ditch. Before the race, I had heard officials say that roads which might be taken in error would not be wired within a certain number of yards, so I was right to think there was no danger!*

Selwyn Edge had sped well clear of such trouble. A bare seven minutes after Foxhall-Keane's departure, he streaked down the long straight to Ballyshannon and the end of a pristine first lap. The *Daily Mail* recorded his arrival at 8.23 — a full ten minutes ahead of schedule. 'A speck appeared over the edge of the distance, and in a flash Edge's Napier came up, and went roaring by with its two crouched, wind-blown occupants, and was gone in a whirl of dust. The speed was terrific, and the one glimpse one had of Edge showed a man with an adamant face clinging like steel to his steering-wheel.'

Aghast at his pace, spectators hurled cheers at the Napier as it leaped across the bumps, its driver bouncing up and down like a jockey, and headed for Kilcullen and the longer western circuit. The narrowness of the road accentuated the impression of speed. Stand viewers looked fearfully through the planks, as they realised for the first time the reality of a Gordon Bennett motor race. One of them remarked 'The speed looked awful, as with a wave of his hand, Edge screamed by and over the rough ground below the grandstand. The staggering of the steering wheels made one's blood run cold.'

*De Knyff completes opening lap (Winton in the background).*

Behind Edge, another drama was unfolding. Twenty minutes later, as Percy Owen approached the finish line, he was observed looking back anxiously at the rising dust which once more denoted the fast-gaining Jenatzy. The number three car was quick enough once it got up to speed with its one gear, but it was no match for the Jenatzy-powered Mercedes. Dropping down the narrow incline towards the grandstand, the Belgian took huge chunks out of the gap between the cars. By the startline, he was on Owen's tail.

The pair presented a startling contrast: Owen jutting professorially out of his flying bedstead, Jenatzy crouched purposefully in the more predatory Mercedes, his anxious mechanic, Fritz Walker, holding on for dear life. The crowd cheered wildly as Jenatzy waved even more furiously. Suddenly, there were three cars on the narrow road together, as the American moved to the right to avoid Winton's stricken car. Jenatzy's Mercedes fishtailed at unabated speed towards the gutter in a cloud of dust and pebbles. Memories of the recent French disaster flashed through many minds — a collision seemed inevitable.

The *Automobile Club Journal* wrote:

*Jenatzy, wild and excited, looked like a man possessed — withal a demon of speed incarnate. He shouted; he nearly stood up in his car; he raised his arms alternately in wild gesticulation. The whole lasted but fifteen seconds but it was a rousing sight and dramatic to a degree. It was the sight of the day, specially reserved for the Ballyshannon enclosure.*

Fortunately, the road widened and with its horn blowing loudly, the Mercedes swept past Owen on the approach to Thomastown stand. 'A hundred yards from the stand, the German car ran in close on the right side and, taking advantage of the slight swerve back towards the left by the American, with a tremendous whirl of machinery it leaped forward and for about four seconds the cars ran alongside. Rapidly, Jenatzy shot ahead and became lost in a cloud of dust, leaving spellbound spectators to slowly recover from the stunning effects.'

Jenatzy said afterwards 'It was my most exciting moment of the entire race.' An opinion with which the shaken American would likely have concurred, as he fought to correct his car which had also taken to the dirt!

The excitement seemed to shock the second Winton into life. No sooner had Jenazy and Owen disappeared, than it gave a few preliminary coughs. A volley of exhaust explosions followed and the engine finally burst into full song at 8.50. Spectators applauded the tired and grimy Alexander Winton and Armstrong as they finally staggered away on their recalcitrant single-geared machine. With 40 minutes lost, they started their first lap while most drivers were commencing their second. Worried that someone might fall on to the track below, the RIC strengthened its numbers at the elevated Club Enclosure fence to which excited spectators had rushed each time a car raced through the grandstand cutting.

Three minutes later Jarrott swept past to another fine reception. It was clear by the instant cessation of dust as the Napier driver approached the line, that the Westrumite was doing a fine job. The closely-following Fernand Gabriel had an anxious moment, when his car swerved violently as he approached the Moat of Ardscull — not something he wanted, as he fought a private duel with Jarrott who had narrowly beaten him in the previous year's Circuit des Ardennes. He leaped out and spent several minutes anxiously checking the axle and wheels. The crowd which had materialised from an adjacent field scattered as he took off again at speed. The Mors skidded wildly and his mechanic Marriage's legs flew out as the Frenchman took the right-hand curve too quickly before he straightened out for the fast run up to Ballyshannon. Gabriel's car was the noisiest in the race. The ground and grandstand shook as it thundered past on full song.

Mooers' Athy delay promoted the final three competitors in road order. Baron de Caters was next to arrive. Despite his pace, he found time for a reassuring wave to his wife. Hot on his heels came Henry Farman, who had confidently lapped faster than any of his compatriots, only a minute slower than Selwyn Edge. But those grandstand spectators who celebrated Edge's spectacular pace and his early demolition of the cream of Europe's drivers were in for a surprise. It was the last driver over the line, the underrated Foxhall-Keene, who took 20 seconds off Edge's time to lead the big race! The 33-year old playboy had outfoxed the professionals — 'Now we know why he's called Foxie!' a spectator commented. His time of 46m.03s. represented an average of 52.2 mph, an incredible speed on such narrow and indifferently surfaced roads.

*'Don't look now!'*
*The Red Devil bears*
*down on Percy Owen.*

Less than three minutes covered the first five drivers at the end of the opening lap, with Edge and Farman just ahead of Charles Jarrott and Camille Jenatzy. The progress of Edge and Jarrott suggested that the English were well on course to retain the Gordon Bennett Cup. But it would take the opening lap of the longer western circuit before a more educated forecast could be made. Was Foxhall-Keene's speed a lucky amateur's flash in the pan? Were the experienced French putting reliability before pace in a more sensible approach to the 327-mile marathon? Would the veteran de Knyff make his move this lap? And what about Red Devil Jenatzy, who had aroused excitement wherever he had appeared? For the Athy-based *Automobile Journal* reporter, he was already the most exciting man in the race, for the manner in which 'the demon of automobilism, skids into the control. The German occupies all our attention. He is the most fascinating of the competitors.'

LAP TIMES: FOXHALL-KEENE 46M.03S., EDGE 46M.23S.,
FARMAN 47M. 31S., JARROTT 48M.14S., JENATZY 48M.58S.,
DE KNYFF 49M.47S.,DE CATERS 52M.17S., GABRIEL 53M10S.,
OWEN 56M57S., WINTON 1H.45M.24S., MOOERS 2H.01M.10S.

# 12 Jarrott Somersaults to Destruction

Sergeant Halley's comet — Napier driver and mechanic left for dead — de Caters' chivalry — Mors revels in Curragh's unrestricted space

## LAP TWO (Western Circuit)

The earlier chilly air was now warming under a hesitant sun. So was the pace, as drivers got down to business after their introductory lap. The sharp note of an army bugle pierced the Curragh morning and alerted expectant spectators to the first arrival on the western circuit. Camille Jenatzy opened the second round on a typical note. He was shouted at by officials for driving too quickly into the Kilcullen control. Here, until experience prevailed, the head marshal had bravely stood in the centre of the road to stop the cars with his red flag!

Edge commenced the lap just after 8.30 as authoritatively as he had completed his first. Faster than the fleetest thoroughbreds Kildare had ever seen, he shed the miles in the car whose colour mirrored that of the Curragh grass which rippled in his speedy wake. The *Irish Field* graphically reported the first stirring sighting of his Napier; 'A flashing streak of green with a comet-like tail of dust behind it appeared, flashed under the green flag, steadied for the curve, and then went roaring across the plain.'

*De Caters at Kildare control stop.*

Two thousand spectators who had arrived by special trains, and as many locals, greeted Edge's triumphant arrival at Kildare. But it was to be the last tubercular flash of British glory. His car's radiator cap flew off soon afterwards and Edge lost precious minutes before he retrieved it. The cap then finally disappeared for good and the engine began to overheat. The radiator sent out jets of steam which had grown to a cloud by the time the unlucky driver reached Monasterevin at nine.

As he wiped the congealing dust from his goggles, the Napier leader confirmed that the car's fanbelt had fallen off. He and his cousin used a towel to bind the radiator filling tube. Had the fan been chain-driven, there would have been no such problem. But Edge was made of stronger material than those fragile car parts and he did not complain. 'The roads are in good order,' he reiterated with Balaclavan fortitude, as he departed in the midst of the steam which issued as if from a volcanic geyser.

Buoyed up after finding that he was taking time out of Camille Jenatzy, Charles Jarrott then picked up the mantle from Edge. 'I was feeling contented and happy and in a very good driving mood,' he later recalled. 'And as I ran into the Kildare control, having begun to really settle down, I almost came to the conclusion that we were going to be well in it at the finish!'

But Jarrott's hopes and the first-lap promise of the English team were about to further fade. His Napier's rhythm was rudely interrupted by a misfire two miles outside Kildare. Jarrott quickly traced the problem to a loose plug wire. He had another nervous moment when he almost collected the unevenly surfaced bridge while exiting Monasterevin. Masterful correction saved the day and he powered past the forests that lined the Maryboro road, even more determined to make up time and realise his ambition of retaining the Gordon Bennett Cup for England. 'No one had a better chance of winning on the following day as myself,' he had written the previous night.

The English didn't have a monopoly of Pandora's box. Only his rapid reflexes saved the focused Farman, when a tyre flew off at speed. Then his car started to lose water and equally essential time with overheating, a possible result of using that substitute pump. The French driver looked exhausted as he struggled into Monasterevin at ten o'clock, having wasted more minutes crossing a field to procure water coolant. 'Water! Water!' was also Louis Mooers' sibilant cry, as he entered Kildare control. He lost another half an hour with overheating down the road at Maryboro, following which his car was reported to be lying unattended in a ditch outside the town.

Although the Curragh's treeless plains were a long remove from the poplar-lined Routes Nationales of its Paris–Madrid success, Gabriel's versatile Mors simply revelled in the unencumbered space. The number six machine shook the window panes in Kildare and Monasterevin as it thundered up the road. The heads of its driver and mechanic were barely visible over top of the race's most streamlined car. Though steeped in military history, Kildare spectators had never seen a missile as awesomely powerful as what they called 'Gabriel's torpedo ship.'

The device lived up to its appearance, time checks showing that it was lapping faster than most of its rivals. Gabriel was literally flying. He took Simmons Corner on two wheels and on his descent to Athy a journalist noted 'he had all four wheels in the air and flew like a projectile for twenty yards.' He had a narrow escape at Jarrott's favourite Monasterevin canal bridge and then slid wide on to the grass at Bloomfield Cross — but he was seen still changing up a gear as he bounded across the gullies!

Camille Jenatzy was also progressing rapidly. The Belgian was feeling increasingly confident with the Mercedes, whose sister car had performed so well in the Paris–Madrid before it ingested the fly. He threw the machine around like no other driver and, as it responded, his assurance grew. He even bent the corners to his will, powersliding around rather than turning. He sped towards Athy and his Leinster Arms fan club in clouds of blue smoke and flashing exhausts. Head marshal Bernard Redwood recorded 'Few will forget the sight, the avalanche of tremendous reports from the engine, and great flames shooting out of the exhaust suggesting a condensed edition of *The Inferno!*'

*Gabriel sets fastest lap at 51 mph.*

It was just after half past nine, when a cloud of dust over the distant green trees signalled the approach to Athy of the first competitor from the western circuit. Selwyn Edge bounced down the hill before stopping neatly within the white lines. His rag-adorned and less than neat Napier was now, however, the real inferno of the race, the engine having overheated to an alarming degree. Though his determined driving had minimised the loss of time, Edge appeared drawn and nervous. He'd had a hard run, during which the constant stream of steam had made the lap a hot-shower nightmare for him and his mechanic cousin, Cecil Edge.

Soon afterwards, Rene de Knyff raced into town. He said he had to contend with a strong headwind for most of the lap and that the road surface did not permit maximum speed. The equanimity of Edge's Napier pit-crew was in sharp contrast to the antics of the blue-overalled workers who descended on the Panhard. They flung cans of petrol to his mechanic, who pierced the bottoms with a steel knife to make the petrol flow more quickly into the tank. Even the normally composed de Knyff was not above joining in the excitement. An official said 'He was cool when nothing needed doing — but to see him bury a wrench in the end of a petrol tin was a sight worth going a distance to see.' The French were delighted that their man had gained on Edge, and they shouted encouragement to him as he prepared to leave.

De Knyff then followed Edge, who had already departed for the exit control. The Napier's engine, however, proved so hot that the 1902 winner could not start the car. In the excitement, he forgot that race rules precluded outside help and he allowed the car to be pushed by eager helpers. De Knyff's pilot cyclist was an Edge fan and he returned to announce sadly that the French had complained about Edge's action. Now, it seemed as if it was down to one man to retain the Cup for England.

With Stocks out, all eyes were now turned up the road in expectation of Charles Jarrott, who with Edge had come to be regarded as a local hero. The experienced Englishman would surely repel the growing French threat. But there was to be no further sighting of the Napier driver — for he had just had a horrific accident while two miles from Stradbally on the Dunamase side. The car's steering failed as he sped down Rock Hill, where local lady Miss Weldon was killed when her horses ran out of control on the gradient.

This section was patrolled by Gorey RIC Sergeant Halley. He explained:

*Shortly after de Knyff passed, we heard the noise of the next car. It was Mr. Jarrott in a green Napier. He was flying down at over 70 mph, when the car suddenly swayed and wobbled violently for over 150 yards, before striking the embankment and then rebounding back on to the road. By the time it was opposite us, the driver seemed to be working desperately to save it, but the car struck the bank again and ran up on it, tearing a swathe of grass completely off for about 30 feet. It then somersaulted into mid-air, throwing Mr. Jarrott out. The entire rear bodywork was torn off, including the petrol tank. I immediately got the red flag to stop the race, before the next competitor would come.*

When the dust cloud cleared, spectators saw Jarrott lying on the road and his mechanic's legs protruding from the upturned wreckage of the number five car. Though clearly stunned and bleeding, Jarrott called to spectators to help him lift the car off Bianchi. Trapped by his safety strap, the mechanic was crying out that the hot exhaust was burning him. After cutting Bianchi loose with a knife, Jarrott and a spectator, Joseph Dobbs of Abbeyleix, laid him by the side of the road.

The car was no sooner manhandled into the ditch than Jarrott returned to the middle of the road. 'I want to go back to my car,' he said.

*Jarrott's Napier immediately after the accident.*

'Your car is finished,' insisted Sergeant Halley, who led him back to the grass bank. The efficient sergeant ensured that the road was quickly cleared of debris. He furled the red flag just as Gabriel thundered downhill, a bare six minutes after the accident.

Baron de Caters was next on the scene. He slowed down in reaction to the crowd. He was past the wreckage before he saw Jarrott, with his clothes torn and blood streaming down his face. He braked hard and reversed back to him. 'Can I do anything for you, can I take you on?' he shouted above the roar of the Mercedes engine.

'No! Where are you going to, what are you doing here?' asked the dazed Jarrott.

'I am racing,' de Caters replied. 'Then get on, man, for goodness sake. Get on, I am all right,' Jarrott insisted.

De Caters shouted that he would relay the news of the accident to grandstand officials and he raced off towards Ballyshannon. Jarrott fainted and was carried into the yard of Fingleton's Grange farm. As Jarrott and Bianchi did not move, spectators thought that both men had been mortally injured. They laid them on clean straw and covered them with a pair of white bed sheets.

The Englishman recalled afterwards:

*When I came to, I wondered if I was dead. I could see sunshine and nothing else. With the hand I could move, I tried to scratch away the blur before my eyes, and found it was a sheet. I looked around and saw that I was lying on straw in a farmyard, and beside me was another sheet. I shall never forget the horror of that moment when it occurred to me that under the second sheet lay poor Bianchi dead. I called to him and to my relief he replied. I then asked him the somewhat superfluous question as to whether he was alive. He replied in a faint voice that he was alive but that he felt very bad.*

Dublin doctor Ben Kennedy, who had been spectating nearby, was quickly on the scene. He first attended to the shocked Bianchi. As onlookers held the sheets over the men to shield them from the sun, the doctor next assured Jarrott that though he had suffered severe bruising, his life was not in danger. A local priest provided even more tangible comfort in the form of generous measures of restorative Irish whiskey.

Dr. Lambert Ormsby, the president of the Royal College of Surgeons, arrived shortly afterwards. The official race physician, he very nearly became a race victim himself as he hastened via the side roads to attend to Jarrott. After a wrong turning near Stradbally, he reversed his car on to the circuit just as none other than the Red Devil himself swept down the road. Spectators screamed, a collision seemed inevitable. But the Belgian quickly swerved across to the footpath, cleared Ormsby's car by inches, and regained the circuit to continue his race. 'I have never seen such speed or such reactions,' the shaken doctor insisted.

The siren slopes of Stradbally ensnared a second Napier victim, when a speeding Edge lost a tyre two miles on the opposite side of the town. In less than two laps, it suddenly seemed as if nothing could now retrieve the fortunes of the green team. When Gabriel stopped in Athy at 10.14, a dead linnet trapped in the Mors' radiator, he passed on the news that Jarrott had crashed and that his car was badly damaged. His hasty observation fuelled more rumours than it answered about the condition of Jarrott and Bianchi. Louis Mooers, meantime, was back on the road again — having tried to cure a sliding fanbelt by sprinkling clay on the flywheel! Long after the other competitors had left, he then inexplicably sped through the Stradbally control.

While Winton still struggled around on his opening eastern circuit lap, Percy Owen was the only American to run competitively. But even he was in trouble with an overheated engine in Athy, where he also nearly ran down his cycle escort. The clothes of the Winton driver and his mechanic were covered in dust and mud after wayside repairs. And following his first round promise their fleeter compatriot Foxhall-Keene also fell by the wayside. He tore off a tyre as he rounded a corner too quickly near Donnelly's Hollow, throwing a shocked Willy Luttgen through the hedge. Like many an enthusiast, he was learning the hard way that it was consistency and concentration rather than sheer speed which won motor races.

*Right: Seventeen-year old mechanic Bianchi was left for dead.*

By this time, the dogged Selwyn Edge had steamed past the Moat of Ardscull. His wife was among the huge numbers who cheered him on his way to the nearby start and finish area. But they all sensed that he was suffering and their eyes quickly turned back up the circuit for his pursuers. They knew enough about motor racing to understand that speed took no prisoners. A fast-approaching column of dust confirmed their worst fears. Exactly six minutes later, de Knyff flew by, having clearly gained on the cup-holder. When Jenatzy raced past eighteen minutes after Edge, having started 21 minutes behind him, there was little doubting the foreign threat.

But surely Jarrott would give the foreigners a run for their money? The crowds watched the empty road and waited. And waited in vain, their hopes turning to despair as the Englishman failed to arrive on schedule. The first intimation that grandstand officials had of Jarrott's accident was a telegram from Stradbally which reported 'Jarrott knocked out; send doctor to Stradbally.' Jarrott's sister, who had been waiting to see him pass her vantage point near Athy, fainted on hearing the news. As she was taken back to Rheban Castle, the suspense grew. Rumours circulated that both driver and mechanic had been killed.

Luckily, the agony of waiting was short-lived. At 10.50, about twenty minutes after the English driver's expected arrival, Baron de Caters surprised the stand audience by pulling up his Mercedes opposite the Ballyshannon timekeepers' tent. As he raised his goggles, spectators were filled with a strange foreboding. The animated stand area fell suddenly quiet. Anxious race stewards surrounded his car. The Baron quickly gave them details of the accident and of Jarrott's injuries. Disappointed that the last English hope had retired, officials were relieved that at least he and Bianchi were alive.

The news was relayed to spectators by the timekeeper, Harry Swindley. They reacted with prolonged applause for the gallant de Caters, as he restarted with difficulty on the slight incline. He was to be cheered every time he subsequently passed the grandstand. The Belgian had sacrificed at least six minutes of valuable racing time on those two stops. News of an accident was something that Baroness de Caters could have done without. But it was worse for Charles Jarrott's sister, who had to wait for six long hours before she heard the welcome report of her brother's survival.

As Camille Jenatzy turned on the heat in his Mercedes, all eyes were on the flying Fernand Gabriel. His 'torpedo ship' justified its lusty presence with the fastest lap time of 60m.19s. (51.7 mph), a minute quicker than the spectacular Jenatzy. The Belgian in turn was a minute faster than the steady Rene de Knyff, who had enjoyed a more trouble-free lap than his team-mate, Farman. As Jenatzy passed the grandstand at 60 mph, he frightened onlookers and officials by waving both hands in the air. Spectators only discovered why when the surprise news came through that his quick time had propelled him into the lead from his lowly fifth on the opening lap.

On aggregate time, the Belgian had two minutes to spare over de Knyff. Edge hung gallantly on to third place a further minute in arrears. Gabriel was a similar distance behind in fourth. There was no doubt as to the speed of either the Breton or his Mors. Buoyed up by his Paris–Madrid success, was Jenatzy's favourite for race honours now preparing to challenge him for the lead? Despite his overheating problems, Farman was fifth ahead of de Caters, whose sportsmanship had cost him at least two places. But for the exuberance which lost him over 20 minutes, Foxhall-Keene might have retained the lead, instead of dropping to seventh behind de Caters. The opening three hours had indeed been eventful.

LAP TIMES: Gabriel 1h.00m.19s., Jenatzy 1h.01m.19s., de Knyff 1h.02m.31s., Edge 1h.07m.03s., de Caters 1h.08m.42s., Farman 1h.10m.27s., Owen 1h.15m.26s., Foxhall-Keene 1h.24m.08s., Winton 2h.34m.26s.

OVERALL TIMES: Jenatzy 1h.50m.17s., de Knyff 1h.52m.18s., Edge 1h.53m.26s., Gabriel 1h.53m.29s., Farman 1h.57m.58s., de Caters 2h.0m.59s., Foxhall-Keane 2h.10m.11s., Owen 2h.12m.23s., Winton 4h.19m.50s.

*Gallant husband, fretting wife. Baroness Axeline de Caters.*

## 13 Farman, de Knyff, and Jenatzy Duel

Axle failure foils Foxhall-Keene — Edge shines in adversity —
Gabriel plagued by misfire — Mooers jousts with hedge and mechanic

## LAP THREE (Eastern Circuit)

Selwyn Edge still led the Gordon Bennett Cup on the road. He showed great courage in continuing to race. He knew he could be next to suffer the steering failure experienced by Jarrott — which had also impelled fellow-Napier driver Mark Mayhew into a tree during the Paris–Madrid event. But one did not, however, become a racing driver by dwelling on danger. As a church bell tolled ten o'clock, he picked up his red card at the Kilcullen control and accelerated once more down the now familiar eastern circuit for the third of the seven laps. While de Knyff and Jenatzy remained behind, there was still hope.

But he hadn't gone far, before his Napier experienced the second of the tyre failures which would comprehensively bury his final hopes of retaining the Cup. Endeavouring to regain time, his car leaped into the air at speed as he negotiated Inchagueirtre bridge near Moone. The Napier returned to earth with such an impact that the left rear tyre flew off. Both rear tyres had to be replaced and one wheel rim was so damaged that it took Edge almost half an hour to refit a spare. As he laboured by the side of a thatched cottage, both de Knyff and Jenatzy sped past. The driver of the number one car would not see them again for the duration of the race.

*Another tyre failure thwarts Edge.*

Two down, three to go, de Knyff must have reflected as he led on the road towards Carlow. Competitors were now being buffeted by a cold east wind and the darkening sky forecast an impending storm. The veteran was reasonably sanguine of another success to add to his tally of racing coups. His car was going well and, though the radiator still bore the marks of that wire barrier, the course held no more hidden surprises. The two minutes down on the race-leader were minuscule in the context of the remaining 240 miles. And he would prefer to have Jenatzy ahead of him than his rapid and fast-rising compatriots, Farman and Gabriel. The uncompromising Mercedes driver had shone in so many events only to crash out or destroy his engine. As de Knyff had frequently reminded his friend Charles Jarrott, the most elemental rule of racing was that 'To win, you've first got to finish.'

Soon de Knyff's main rivals were reduced to two. Gabriel started to experience the frustrations of an intermittent fuel supply problem which would cost him any chance of success. The Mors would ask for more speed, but then splutter along as if on three cylinders. 'One minute flying with the wind, the next sulking like that cloud,' a spectator noted. The unpredictable car also caught out its driver at Kilcullen, where he overshot the tricky turn and had difficulty in reversing. There was no grandstand at Castledermot, but the approach hedges were lined with people who marvelled at Gabriel's speed as he swept past them once more on full song. But then the car faltered again, as he entered the town. This caused him to overshoot the control entry and cost another time-consuming reversal. As the Breton dashed away from the inconsolable Mors mechanics, he cried *'C'est impossible.'* Foxhall-Keene's German mechanic said something similar in English when he complained of axle trouble and his driver, however, insisted they race on.

Sweeping imperiously past Ballymoon corner which he had overshot first time around, Rene de Knyff must have reflected wryly on the mistake without which he might now be leading Jenatzy instead of following him. But the corner should claim no more victims. Once he had recovered from his accident shock, Stocks had asked the police not to replace the wire, since at any moment another driver might also run out of road. They however, firmly demurred — 'otherwise it will not be fair to the drivers who had already passed!'

The Napier driver sent a special messenger to the Carlow police who finally gave instructions to undo the wire. And a good job for Henry Farman that he did. No sooner had the wire been removed than the Panhard driver arrived far too quickly to take the corner. Henry Bruen's grandstand spectators had another treat, as he followed in the wheelmarks of de Knyff and Stocks. But with no wire to ensnare him he just as quickly reversed and was gone, while onlookers still marvelled at his unscheduled arrival.

Athy spectators were disappointed when Selwyn Edge failed to arrive on schedule. Then they learned that he had lost another tyre outside Carlow, the cover flying along the straight road for twenty yards to the amazement of rural viewers. But they gave a warm reception to de Knyff, the first to race into the town at 11 o'clock. Twelve minutes later, Jenatzy arrived. His frenetic pace made de Knyff's entrance seem pedestrian. The German personnel were by now equally fired up. They splashed both the Belgian and his mechanic as they doused the hot Mercedes tyres with cold water. They checked what looked like a slight tear on the rear offside cover, before allowing him to leave.

Jenatzy's take-off left no doubt as to his determination to consolidate his lead. Spectators all around the course gasped at his spectacular cornering. Before his own crash, Charles Jarrott enjoyed a rare and apprehensive bird's-eye view of the Belgian at work.

> *It was after he left me in Carlow that I had an opportunity of seeing how he was driving. The road was very winding and Jenatzy went 'all-out'. Some of his skids on the corners were hair-raising, and he missed several stone walls by only a fraction, judging by his wheelmarks. I did not think it possible that he could continue to take such risks and survive. De Knyff evidently thought the same.*

Jenatzy's determination was matched by Selwyn Edge's perseverance. Aware of his fight against the odds, the Athy crowd applauded the Napier driver when he finally arrived twenty five minutes afterwards. Looking none the worse for his spectacular race exit, J.W. Stocks was also on hand to greet his team-mate. The presence of both men was considered something of a miracle by a section of the crowd — each having earlier been reported killed! But the English team drivers knew that nothing short of a real miracle would now retain the Gordon Bennett Cup. Edge sipped an appropriately cold tea before cleaning his goggles and restarting.

By contrast, Fernand Gabriel's Mors was once more on full song. The birdcatcher raced into the control just before midday, this time sporting the remains of an ill-fated sparrow. Blue-overalled mechanics fussed around the car but they still failed to find the cause of the misfire which some erroneously thought to be electrical. They checked the carburettor and all the connections. Sadly, they didn't inspect the apparently inoffensive cork with which they had earlier replaced an ill-fitting tank cap.

By this time, news of Baron de Caters' sportsmanship had reached Athy. He received a hero's reception when he arrived two minutes after midday. The Mercedes driver was proving to be one of the most consistent competitors. His times were only slightly slower than those of such professionals as Jenatzy and de Knyff. Henry Farman was happier this time around, his car once more performing perfectly after its earlier overheating problems.

James Foxhall-Keane again astounded his team by matching the pace of the more experienced drivers. But just before Athy, he struck an embankment and mechanics warned him against continuing when they noticed an ominous crack in the back axle near the driving wheel. Foxhall-Keene asked a control official if he should continue. 'For heaven's sake, no!' the man replied.

*Cooling the tyres of the chivalrous Baron de Caters.*

'I'll try for a few more miles!' the American said cheerfully. 'He want kill me!' Willy Luttgen was heard to say, as they set off tentatively to complete the lap at Ballyshannon.

There was to be no such reprieve, however, for Louis Mooers. He ran through the Athy western control at 12.30 — still on his first western circuit lap! It was likely that he hadn't stopped as his stricken car might prove impossible to restart. An eventful five hours had taught him that the racetrack was infinitely more stressful than the drawing office. On one occasion, he dramatically ripped open the car's bonnet with a knife, in his haste to solve its overheating problems. He argued with his mechanic over a recurrent gear selection problem. Then, the front offside tyre fell off on a sharp corner and he crashed into a hedge and damaged a wheel.

Almost thankfully, the Clevelander finally parked the less than Peerless car in a side road outside Athy. It remained under an RIC man's watchful eye for the duration of the race, leaving Owen and Winton to carry the flag for the United States. Though this proved to be his best lap, the oil-stained Winton was still way off the leaders' pace in his over-heating car. The equally weary Percy Owen was even further behind, trying to coax a car which a reporter said had 'overheated like a furnace.'

Ballyshannon grandstand provided one of the most exciting views of the cars at speed. One awed reporter wrote:

> When the great cars leaped and thundered beneath us, the impression was like that produced by the fleeting view one gets when the countryside is

*Hard day at the office, Mooers parks his less than Peerless car.*

*illuminated on a dark night by brilliant flashes of lightning. We'd hardly seen the cars at the moment they flashed by, and yet they were indelibly printed on the mind, and the picture stands before one by day and night as a thing marvellous, incomprehensible, unique.*

While awaiting the flashing cars, grandstand spectators were further entertained by the music of the band of the 11th Hussars — but it was accepted that they could desert their instruments when the cry went up 'Car coming!' Their brass instruments glinting in the sun, the band played the national anthem when the Lord Lieutenant, the Earl of Dudley, arrived with his party at 11.30. According to the London *Times*, the grandstand accommodated the most cosmopolitan crowd ever seen in Ireland. The number of foreigners easily equalled that of the English and Irish, and they were predominantly French.

Stand guests included Charley Lehmann, the Parisian Mercedes agent who had secured the German team cars, and Gordon Bennett's personal representative, Mr. Mitchell. Also Wicklow's Charles Segrave, whose son, Henry, was destined to become the fastest man in the world on land, water and in the air. An English visitor was surprised to observe another distraction — 'A couple of Rouge et Noir tables, where gambling was carried on at a brisk pace right under a constable's eye!' The nearby *Autocar*'s balloon provided further diversion, as it defied all efforts at inflation in the rising wind. Eighty cylinders of unused hydrogen stood forlornly in the field, as the balloon's traction engine bogged down in sympathy. But the machine more than redeemed itself by conscientiously alerting spectators to approaching cars with a regular distinctive Toot.

The worst fears of English supporters were soon to be realised as the signal to mark the end of the lap heralded the arrival, not of Selwyn Edge, but of his rival, Rene de Knyff. These two drivers were the most easily recognisable on the course, de Knyff because of his bulk and Edge on account of his white coat. The Britons nevertheless sportingly saluted the Panhard driver as he raced past at full speed, to be soon followed by Jenatzy's equally healthy Mercedes. It was an indication of Edge's problems that he did not arrive until half an hour later. Even French supporters also encouraged him, as the hissing Napier finally passed just ahead of Gabriel. Edge pointed to his wheels to explain his delay. Among those rooting for the Napier man was Derby-winning Bruree horse trainer John Gubbins, who cautioned, 'The race is never over 'til they cross the line!'

It was only when times were finally collated that spectators knew the exact time differences. There were more French *bravos* when it was clear that Farman had set the fastest lap of 49 minutes and 35 seconds, ten seconds quicker than Jenatzy. De Knyff was third, a further minute in arrears. Not once forgetting to wave to his worrying wife, Baron de Caters once again showed his class with fourth best time of 51 minutes and 11 seconds. Amazingly, Foxhall-Keene was only three seconds slower, despite his confrontation with the embankment! There was no doubting his speed or courage, but the axle fracture was worsening. To the chagrin of Luttgen he insisted 'We will see how she holds out to Kilcullen.'

*Below:*
*Irish and martial airs for grandstand spectators.*

'The Franco-German war is on again!' a journalist proclaimed, as it became apparent that a battle royal was looming between the French and Germans. With their team still complete, the former looked a likely bet for success as they enfiladed Jenatzy in the most competitive Mercedes. But despite their pressure, the Red Devil had increased his lead by a minute to three minutes over de Knyff, who it seemed was still keeping his powder dry. Would he shed his legendary imperturbability on the next lap, and would Jenatzy finally fall on his sword?

The French challenge looked even stronger when Mercedes lost the stout defender, Foxhall-Keene. His broken axle finally forced a reluctant retreat from the fray at nearby Kilcullen. Despite his problems, the amiable Irish-American didn't lose his sense of humour. Having learnt that his horse *Conroy 11* was running in England, a spectator asked him what were its chances. 'About as much chance as I have!' the Mercedes driver laughed; the horse eventually did better than its owner, finishing sixth. (Later, Foxhall-Keene brought Willy Luttgen to the United States, where he graduated to driving and contested the inaugural Vanderbilt Cup Race.)

LAP TIMES: FARMAN 49M.35S., JENATZY 49M.45S., DE KNYFF 50M.57S., DE CATERS 51M.11S., FOXHALL-KEANE 51M.14S., GABRIEL 1H.2M.37S., WINTON 1H.7M.37S., EDGE 1H.27M.59S., OWEN 4H.41.24S.

OVERALL TIMES: JENATZY 2H.40M.02S., DE KNYFF 2H.43M.15S., FARMAN 2H.47M.33S., DE CATERS 2H.52M.10S., GABRIEL 2H.56M.06S., FOXHALL-KEENE 3H.1M.25S., EDGE 3H.21M.25S., WINTON 5H.27M.27S., OWEN 6H.53M.47S.

## 14  Band Plays on as Storm Batters Drivers

Gabriel spins — cheers for Edge and Winton — accident rumours — web-footed Jenatzy increases lead

## LAP FOUR (Western Circuit)

A new factor rudely invaded the race. Heavy clouds had gradually replaced the reluctant morning sunshine. They suddenly gave vent to a violent storm shortly after midday. Control banners flapped and rain beat a fearsome tattoo on marquee roofs. Competitors winced at the bitter wind-blown onslaught which reduced vision and made the roads treacherously slippy.

Some of the narrower straights became corners, drivers had to fight continually to check their machines on the shifting surface. Gateways and open spaces hid additional hazards, unpredictable gusts which threatened to wrest cars off the track. It was as if nature was going to show these twentieth-century mechanical interlopers who was the real boss. Thunder reverberated across the Curragh and from Kildare to Athy and Carlow, its reports mimicking those of the petrol-fired monsters which up to now had dominated the midlands morning. The heart of Baron de Caters' wife beat faster. She felt even more isolated among strangers in the cold stand, while her husband was risking his life out on that dangerous course which had already claimed victims.

The storm was well timed for the grandstand viewers, who adjourned en masse to the lunch tents. Like the Titanic orchestra, the rain-soaked Hussars stoically continued their selection of Irish and international airs. Another eating marathon took place at the Moat of Ardscull, where over a thousand lunches were served in race-matching time. The congregation numbered 3,000, a third of whom had camped there the preceding night. It included the biggest-ever assembly of British and Irish cycling and motoring trade representatives.

They savoured the headiest gossip and surmise. Wild rumours filtered through that Edge had been killed and that Stocks had gone over a bridge at Carlow. By the time this news reached the enclosure's opposite side, Stocks had reportedly demolished the bridge and been killed with his mechanic. Jarrott had likewise been variously assassinated long before lunchtime, once

*Not dead, just wounded. The indomitable Selwyn Edge leaves Athy control.*

after a dramatic Maryboro collision with Jenatzy! But the Moat spelt genuine bad news for the character who rashly arrived on the cycle which he had previously pinched from an *Irish Wheelman* employee. The bike was recognised by its former owner. The culprit's race involvement lasted little longer than Charles Jarrott's.

The storm continued. This fourth lap was one that drivers would not forget in a hurry. With no dry-tented shelter, their faces were soon raw red as they raced into the cold midday rain which, at 60 mph, peppered their faces with the impact of giant hailstones. The downpour which had at first put a welcome dampener on the ubiquitous dust now made driving a misery on the open mudguardless machines. The track wavered under the cars' speeding wheels. Competitors reported that the stretch between Athy and Ballyshannon was in a particularly bad state, with a treacherous oily surface.

'When the cars were out of sight, one shuddered for the racers' safety over the winding roads in the blinding rain,' a journalist observed. The rain and distant mist also considerably reduced visibility from the Moat of Ardscull. But despite spectators' most earnest speculation, the hostile elements only slightly slowed the fearless competitors. With so much at stake, it seemed as if it would take more than a storm to eclipse these new-age warriors in their space-reducing wonders. As a spray of wet flints replaced the dust, they raced on, apparently impervious to the rivulets which ran down their necks and the mud that the wheels flung directly into their faces.

Camille Jenatzy appeared to be most at home with his car. Robust he might not be, but this day he was riding high above whatever arrows the weather or his fellow-competitors could throw at him. He continued to throw the Mercedes around with apparent but precise abandon. Though he frightened spectators he revelled in the conditions which suited his sliding style and he quickly found his limits. There was a bend after Ballyshannon which he regularly took faster than any of his rivals, deliberately running his offside wheels up the grassy bank in order to gain a faster exit for the straight run down to Kilcullen. Future racer Sammy Davis observed 'When he comes into the corners, it's like there are three or four Jenatzys trying to get around. His motto must be "if you are not sideways, you are not trying"!'

French hopes that the conditions would restrain the Mercedes driver were severely dashed. Reports from around the circuit soon confirmed that he was in fact increasing his three-minute lead! Though Henry Farman had impressed with his fast times, race experts insisted that it would be the veteran de Knyff who would mount the most serious challenge to the determined Jenatzy. But when de Knyff entered Athy for the fourth time at 12.42, Jenatzy was only six minutes behind him on the road, having increased his lead by almost eight minutes

The contrast between the two compatriots could hardly be greater. Outside the controls, Jenatzy seldom left his car. He waited impatiently, throwing up his hands and gesticulating at the slightest provocation. An Athy marshal described his arrival technique. Jenatzy drove 'hard at top speed right up to the entrance to the control. Bang went all the brakes, the back wheels locked, and after a marvellous skid of exactly 32 yards his car came to rest between the white lines.'

His Panhard rival was invariably relaxed, even though the pressure was on him to bridge that increasing gap. 'De Knyff threw out his clutch six yards from the control, and ran his car right in with its own momentum. He left neat lines as straight as an arrow, while Jenatzy's marks were always a zigzag.' The French team leader undoubtedly conserved his tyres but it was at the expense of precious time. A loss of even four seconds per inward control would cost over three minutes by the end of the race.

The storm eased but there was little harmony on the roads. The competition intensified even further between the French pack and the lone German hare. And Farman was also hot on the heels of de Knyff. After his blistering opening western lap, the French were also hoping that Fernand Gabriel and his Mors would now take some real time out of Jenatzy.

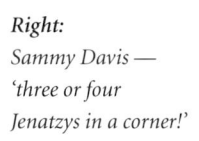

*Right:*
*Sammy Davis —*
*'three or four*
*Jenatzys in a corner!'*

Although his engine was still not running perfectly, Gabriel made full use of its power over the early miles. It was obvious that he was trying when he enlivened the Kildare proceedings by completely misjudging his approach to the inward control. He spun on the drying road and then overshot the line and lost extra seconds while reversing. The temperamental car was misfiring again — but by the time Gabriel reached Athy, it was once more running perfectly! Despite the delays, the Breton hadn't entirely given up hope, and he was only slightly off the pace of the favourites Jenatzy and de Knyff. Sadly, it wasn't to be until after the race that his team would identify the minor problem which had caused such frustration.

No sooner had Gabriel left Athy, than Baron de Caters raced in to another warm welcome. Unlike Gabriel, he was enjoying his so far trouble-free race. He calmly lit a cigarette while awaiting the signal to restart. There was generous support too for the determined Winton, when he arrived with a long strip of aluminium hanging from below his badly overheated car. And even louder cheers for Selwyn Edge — who had been reported killed in a Monasterevin accident! The Napier driver explained that he had lost another tyre there, as well as having to be push-started because of overheating. But though conscious of being out of the running, his rapid departure clearly demonstrated that he had no intention of retiring. He frightened spectators as he skidded the steaming Napier around the Moat at almost impossible speed in his efforts to make up ground.

*Restless Jenatzy frets at a control stop.*

Meantime, there was consternation back at the grandstand. A telegram from Maryboro suggested that race-leader Jenatzy and the dashing Fernand Gabriel had been involved in a collision and that many people had been injured. Was the race to end in another disaster, like Paris–Madrid? Wise French heads nodded, they had said all along that Jenatzy was never to be a winner. De Knyff would triumph again. But what of their man Gabriel? One scribe was now feeling guilty for having written that the Breton 'drove with the recklessness of a Soudanese going into battle!'

The minutes grew heavy. Their pocket-watch hands seemed to be immobile, as the crowds anxiously awaited the first cars to complete the fourth lap. Then, a counter rumour gathered happier momentum. The first message had been a ghastly mistake. When the traction engine finally signalled an arrival at one o'clock, grandstand and finish line spectators rushed to the fence with renewed excitement. 'It's number two!' someone shouted. It was de Knyff and his blue Panhard as expected. But whose was that rapidly growing dust cloud travelling fast in his wake from Athy?

It was a very much alive and astonishingly quick Jenatzy, who was now only four minutes behind de Knyff on the road. So great was the relief at the Belgian's sighting, that even the French waved their hats to their most feared opponent. But the indestructible Red Devil had clearly increased his lead. This could be the turning point of the race, which had developed into a contest between the gourmet and the hungry second-generation immigrant.

*Calm de Knyff enjoys a sandwich.*

Already contemplating retirement, the refined de Knyff had a lot to live for. Jenatzy invariably lived only when he raced. Was this to be the Red Devil's day? And after surviving for so many years unscathed, had de Knyff's first-lap upsets led him to settle for a more conservative and safer pace? Were Mercedes about to score their first major race success and rearrange the automobile balance of Europe? The debate continued as spectators resumed their seats after having happily greeted the noisy arrival of the second telegram victim, Fernand Gabriel. The fearsome Mors rattled the grandstand planks. Like a child with an outsize toy, its diminutive driver waved with the joy of one again happily motoring on all cylinders.

Once the times were made available it was clear that, barring accidents or mechanical mishap, Jenatzy was indeed now clear favourite. He had made fastest time of 61 minutes and 52 seconds — almost three minutes ahead of anyone else. This had increased the Belgian's lead to ten minutes over de Knyff. With a total disregard for the conditions, and while his main rivals had significantly slowed, he had gone almost as rapidly in the wet as on the dry opening lap! His web-footed mastery clearly demonstrated that it was sheer ability and commitment, rather than engine power, which had so effectively propelled him to the front.

Though two minutes off his previous record time, Gabriel still managed second fastest in 64m.20s, ahead of Farman's 65m.55s. and de Caters who recorded 67m.19s.. The overall first three race places remained the same, but the fleet Farman had halved the four minute gap to the delayed de Knyff in second place. De Caters retained his fourth position almost a minute ahead of the closing Gabriel. Edge was a fading sixth ahead of Winton and Mooers, each of whom was now a lap in arrears.

LAP TIMES: JENATZY 1H.1M.52S., GABRIEL 1H.4M.20S.,
FARMAN 1H.5M.55S., DE CATERS 1H.7M.19S., DE KNYFF 1H.8M.16S.,
OWEN 1H.19.40S., EDGE 1H.24M.59S., WINTON 2H.15M.36S.

OVERALL TIMES: JENATZY 3H.41M.54S., DE KNYFF 3H.51M.31S.,
FARMAN 3H.53M.38S., DE CATERS 3H.59M.29S., GABRIEL 4H.0M.26S.,
EDGE 4H.46M.24S., WINTON 7H.43M.3S., OWEN 8H.13M.27S.

# 15 French Reduce Jenatzy's Lead

Farman's fastest lap — de Caters' consistency — mechanics' courage — de Knyff meets a jaywalker

## LAP FIVE (Eastern Circuit)

A renewed downpour drenched the racers just after one o'clock. Strong gusts of wind threatened the Ballyshannon timekeepers' tent. Spectators peered out from tents and under trees and marvelled as drivers pierced the curtain of rain at almost unabated speed.

But, suddenly, it was as if the storm threw in the towel! One up to the new-age warriors, as the sun warmly triumphed once again. Like Beethoven's *Pastoral*, the umbrellas were furled and sunshades replaced the macintoshes. The washed sky oversaw a happier tempo and the roadside bushes shook themselves free of their wet contents each time a racer whirled past.

Rene de Knyff led the eight remaining cars as he picked up his red card for the last lap of the eastern circuit. The final two laps would be over the western loop. With Jenatzy leading so emphatically, he may have wondered how long it would be before the flying Belgian would compound his defeat by actually passing him on the road as well. The honour of France was at stake, it was time to shed some of that caution. He tightened his steering wheel grip as he raced out of Kilcullen at maximum speed.

Jenatzy took little notice of the times, however, as he turned his mud-spattered Mercedes south. Confident that he now had the measure of his rivals and the still damp circuit, he eased the pace. But not by much! *Motor News* noted:

> *It was an amazing sight to witness him bound over the culverts at top speed. At fifty, he took a flying leap with all four wheels in the air for a moment, and then came down with an appalling smash on the road again. But his steering was as straight as a die, and those sinewy arms with their nerves of steel, held the great machine ever straight to the course. The dark goggles concealed Jenatzy's well-lidded hawks' eyes of jackdaw blue; but the wispish wind-tortured red beard and the hard determined mouth were clearly indicated. His car at high speed leaped along in great undulating strides, and his flapping oilskins swayed up and down in unison.*

The Red Devil would certainly never match the coolness of the impressively fast Farman. While waiting for his departure orders at Carlow control, the Panhard driver found time for a bottle of Bass and a brief promenade! By contrast, slowing down or not, the impatient race-leader jumped out and seized one of the wheels to push his Mercedes to the refuelling area as soon as he arrived at Athy.

The strategic Athy controls were the best policed by team assistants, who were busy for every lap of the 327-mile race. In addition to the excitement of the constant passage of the competitors, spectators enjoyed the rivalry between the highly organised mechanics. They were amazed that the Germans could forecast a Mercedes arrival by a distant engine note. The Germans had painted the name Mercedes on a board marking their area, while a tricolour flapped proudly over the French quarter.

Apart from superintending the tyre and oil supplies, mechanics regularly replenished the large tubs of water in order to cool both thirsty radiators and equally hot tyres. Teams of two men threw the water at the tyres of the still-moving cars, each hit or miss winning an appropriate response from spectators. Some also ran alongside the cars as they handed over oil and petrol, just before the cars crossed the control lines. *Motor News* noted, however, that unlike the well-focused continentals, 'the Americans made a lot of fuss, and it was easy to see that they were newcomers to the game.'

*Moat spectators welcome the sunshine.*

With little team support, the Americans could not match their rivals' professionalism. But no number of mechanics could have helped Winton and Owen. Their badly overheating cars staggered in almost two laps behind the leaders, Winton's machine emitting a salvo of loud explosions. It seemed as if the fledgling American automobile industry lagged far behind that of Europe, despite the *Automobile Topics* boast that 'any one of fifteen makers in America could build a car to win the Trophy.'

This race lap, however, held no such problems for the closely-matched French. Farman and Gabriel were circulating rapidly. The Mors driver bellowed into Athy at 2.27. The *Automotor Journal* reporter suggested that a special word would have to be coined to describe the speed and rush of the powerful car. 'It should be some grand wonderful onomatopoeic word, in which the strength, the panting roar, the effect that it has on the mind of some almost cruel physical torture, the sense of terrific, inhuman speed, is all represented.'

Tortured by neither neology nor fuel starvation, Gabriel's broad smile confirmed that this had been one productive lap. His car was again running almost perfectly. Officials could hardly believe that he was the same person who had so vociferously argued with them on a previous lap. He had left in high dudgeon after not being allowed to save time by tightening a metal casing nut while inside the control area. 'The French can be a little temperamental!' a timekeeper confirmed. This time, Gabriel's team adjusted the valves and re-pumped the tyres outside the control area, as per regulations, before the Mors raced off to Ballyshannon.

Panhard's Henry Farman was as happy as his team-mate. He felt that he had done his best-ever time on the rapid run down from Kilcullen. But his pace was closely matched by the rapid Baron de Caters. Few drivers were as consistent as the unruffled Belgian. 'You could time your clock by him,' said a timekeeper, as the Mercedes driver arrived shortly afterwards right on schedule.

Consistency was what distinguished an excellent driver from a merely good one. Many drivers could do one good time by a mixture of ability and good fortune. But it was the skill and concentration to take each corner perfectly lap after lap which sorted out the men from the boys. On his three laps of the 40-mile eastern circuit de Caters' times varied by only a minute. The difference between two of his western circuit times was three seconds! The millionaire Belgian might neither need nor receive a wage packet, but he was no amateur racer. He had also studied photographs of the circuit long before he arrived in Ireland!

His engine problems may have earlier denied Gabriel such consistency. But his pace was now dramatic and once again the Mors greedily devoured space all around the circuit. His mechanic Mariage was equally spectacular. Observers were shocked to see him reach over the front of the car and make an engine adjustment — while they were travelling at top speed!

The unsung riding mechanics were a breed apart. They endured crouched hours of exposure to the elements and the roar of the huge unsilenced engines.

Their precarious side-steps were only inches away from the menacing chains which transmitted the drive to the rear wheels. Mercedes mechanic, Carl Menzel, was killed during the opening Vanderbilt Cup Race in the United States.

The mechanics' role was to maintain fuel pressure, read the instruments, and assist with repairs or tyre replacement. As mirrors had yet to be thought of, they also had to warn the driver of an approaching car. According to Moore Brabazon, one top French operator always raced athwart a very uncomfortable jack. The man explained 'It's the most vital piece of equipment in the car and it's important that the mechanic always knows where it is!' A *Motor News* correspondent paid these fearless men an overdue tribute: 'Holding on by their eyebrows to a motorcar moving at some fearful speed, they never knew when the least mistake on the part of the driver, or a flaw in the car, would cause sudden and fearful death. I never saw such pluck.'

*Happy again, Gabriel and spectacular Mariage make a control stop.*

Having put welcome time between himself and his Ballymoon fright, Rene de Knyff had once again to call on his reserves of pluck as he passed the crowded Castledermot approaches. A constable had earlier prevented an elderly spectator from going on to the road. But as soon as his back was turned the man resumed his original direction. The RIC officer raced after him, but the miscreant panicked and headed across the footpath — and into the Panhard's path. De Knyff missed him by inches and the man was so unnerved that he flung himself into the thorny hedge. It transpired that he was one of the few addicts who hadn't taken the parish priest's abstinence sermon to heart. Spectators speculated that Rene de Knyff might succeed where the PP had failed.

The hapless Selwyn Edge was the one most in need of strong sustenance. He was now 35 minutes behind Gabriel, having started 35 minutes ahead of him. Not only was the untested Napier a handful to steer but he lost another twenty five minutes with tyres which obstinately refused to stay on the rims at speed. An ironic predicament for a man who had previously insisted that a car could only ever be as good as its tyres. While the Michelin and Clipper Continental covers provided his Mors, Panhard and Mercedes rivals with virtually trouble-free runs, the Napier's tyres were a bad advertisement for Dunlop. The wily Harvey du Cros would have some explaining to do once he returned to the boardroom from his houseboat. Typically, though, his involvement with Panhard ensured that he also had his landlubber's feet in a more successful camp.

The approach to Ballyshannon was undulating. One observer compared an approaching car to a bouncing ball which rolled down the incline and then suddenly jumped again as it hit the bump right under the grandstand, before bounding away freely in the direction of Kilcullen. Only the drivers, however, knew how much effort was required to keep their cars straight on that narrow corrugated section. Rene de Knyff headed the raucous taut playthings as he bounced through Ballyshannon at 2.30 to commence his sixth and second last lap. When Jenatzy followed, it was obvious that he had lost a couple of minutes to the French team leader.

Demonstrating once again what he could do with a well-behaved car, Gabriel also lapped a whole two minutes faster than Jenatzy in 51 minutes and four seconds. Had he not lost so much time earlier, he would now be up with the race-leader. As the Mors driver finished his fifth circuit at three o'clock, he was closely followed by Winton who was completing his third. Fellow-American Owen completed his third lap three-quarters of an hour later at 3.42.

Many thought that Gabriel's would be the best time for the lap. But at 3.20 Farman raced past to record a time which was half a minute inside Gabriel's! It was his second time to take fastest lap. De Caters was an impressive third quickest in 51m. 21s. His wife was happy for his salute, now there were only two laps to go. When all the times had been collected, it was seen that Farman had confirmed his Paris–Vienna form. He had taken no less than two and a half minutes out of Jenatzy's lead and another minute from Rene de Knyff. Would the apprentice overtake his master? Little over a minute covered the first four drivers' lap times, the competition was indeed hotting up.

The fleet French armada had significantly reduced Jenatzy's lead. The Belgian must have regretted his uncharacteristic temperance, as much as de Knyff fretted over his earlier time losses. Without those delays, the Panhard driver would now be only a minute in arrears and well on course to achieving his final ambition of adding the Gordon Bennett Cup to his string of city-to-city successes. 'Maybe, it will be a case of being third time lucky,' he had told journalists before the start. And if the Panhards and Mors could gain so much on the shorter circuit, what inroads might they make over the final two longer laps? Eight minutes was not an impossible margin to reel in.

French correspondents were in a frenzy of excitement. After 200 arduous miles covered by the leaders at over 48 mph, this was one of the closest contests they had ever witnessed. Only 16 minutes overall covered the first five cars. And their drivers were gaining on the race-leader! They earnestly discussed how Jenatzy would react to the pressure of the chase. Would he now finally wilt and fall off? And would the flying Farman do the unthinkable and pass the more experienced de Knyff? Would France have a new racing hero?

The race was far from being decided yet — and the timed mile section revealed how closely matched were the cars. The Mercedes machines of Jenatzy and de Caters had recorded 66 mph, marginally ahead of Farman's and de Kynff's Panhards at 65 mph, and Edge's 64 mph Napier. However, those who doubted Jenatzy's stamina obviously didn't know that, before the race, he had driven the Mercedes all the way from Cannstatt to Le Havre — at near racing speeds! He and the car were familiar and very compatible accomplices.

LAP TIMES: FARMAN 50M.31S., GABRIEL 51M.04S., DE CATERS 51M.21S., DE KNYFF 51M.40S., JENATZY 53M.16S., OWEN 1H.5M.33S., EDGE 1H.14M.35S.

OVERALL TIMES: JENATZY 4H.35M.10S., DE KNYFF 4H.43M.11S., FARMAN 4H.43M.59S., DE CATERS 4H.50M.50S., GABRIEL 4H.51M.30S., EDGE 6H.0M.59S., OWEN 9H.19M.00S.

*The determined Henry Farman sets another fastest lap and closes on de Knyff.*

# 16 The Red Devil Stamps his Authority

Gabriel's equine confrontation — Edge in tyre wars —
Farman overtakes teamleader — Winton flies into retirement

## LAP SIX (WESTERN CIRCUIT)

As soon as he realised the progress of his rivals, Jenatzy immediately resumed his normal and more rapid rate. Restraint and he had never been comfortable cockpit companions. Far from feeling pressure, he was happier and safer driving at his own pace. From this point on, he stamped his authority firmly on the race. He may well have realised that de Knyff was under greater strain, with his team-mate Farman now within 50 seconds of deposing him from second place. As he sped westwards into the crucial sixth circuit, Jenatzy must also have been thanking the second-lap problems which had cost Farman the ten minutes which now separated the pair.

Untroubled by either mechanical or tyre drama, the Belgian equalled Gabriel's record lap pace as he sped across the furze-crowned hillocks of the Curragh just before three o'clock. Eight hours in the driving seat all ready, but he showed no signs of tiring. A Cork-bound train whistled plaintively as he effortlessly outpaced it. He galvanised the Kildare locals as he accelerated downhill into the control, leaving his braking until the last possible moment.

A boy named Sheridan was so excited that he dodged past a Market Square policeman to see the Red Devil follow his cycle escort — and ran straight into the mudguard of a following touring car. The youngster became one of the race's only two briefly hospitalised casualties but, like young Arthur Jones who fell from another arboreal perch, he also escaped with only minor injuries. With the likes of the Red Devil breathing down their necks, the cycle escorts endured an exhausting and hazardous day's work.

A journalist tried to explain Jenatzy's magnetism:

*There is some strange sympathetic likeness between the man and his car. As the Mercedes stands there, its mighty engine panting and straining impotently, while a blue flame flashes from its exhaust, it seems a veritable extract from hell. And Jenatzy fits the Mercedes. The other drivers who passed us were calm, but he is excited — wildly so. To be at rest appears to be for him an almost unbearable physical torture; his face is covered with oil and grease and dust, through which his sunshine complexion stands out; his red moustache and little red beard add the necessary finishing touch to a figure that seems to be the incarnation of the delirium of speed.*

Speed, however, was once more eluding the hapless Fernand Gabriel. Having been two minutes quicker than Jenatzy last time around, this penultimate lap would be a crucial one in realising his reasonable pre-race hopes of repeating his Paris–Madrid success. But the Mors again let him down. Its engine was misfiring badly, as he followed Jenatzy into Kildare. He and Mariage quickly removed and cleaned the carburettor for the fifth frustrating time. And for a second time in the day, the Breton found himself at unexpected eye-level with an Irish quadruped!

A local newspaper explained:

*A man driving a sorry-looking nag, to which was attached an antiquated trap, by some means or another got into the control at the Monasterevin end. He ambled down the street in the direction of the military hutments, and he then stopped. The police shouted and gesticulated, as they endeavoured to warn the man of the danger he was in. Just then, a racing car entered the control, and the placid driver gazed at the blue motor. 'I don't think much of it,' he said to the irate Sergeant who had to hold the horse's head. 'Here's back to Clonbullogue.' And he tried to get back at once, but his name and address had to be entered up!*

*Tour de Stradbally. Bicycle escort leads Paris–Madrid winner Gabriel.*

Ahead of Gabriel and the dissident farmer, Rene de Knyff hammered on towards Stradbally's whitewashed houses and the Sibelian vastness of Windy Gap. Though the Frenchman afterwards admitted that he had left it too late, he speeded up in a last determined effort to regain the Gordon Bennett Cup for France. But his fresh wheelmarks only provided further stimulus for the following Jenatzy. The Belgian was now just a couple of miles behind him on the road, head down and ignoring the antiquity of Dunamase as he made his own history. The Hound of Destiny was finally and firmly by his shoulder. And it was soon very evident that de Knyff indeed had a war on two fronts. Unofficial timings along the route from Ballyshannon to Kildare and Stradbally confirmed that Farman was easily equalling the pace of the leading pair.

Stradbally provided further unwelcome excitement for the French team leader. A misdirected petrol can struck the side of the Panhard and tore a hole near the top of the water tank. This was too much on top of his other dramas. The veteran succumbed to untypical histrionics at the antics of his anxious team. According to *The Irish Times*, 'Liquid flowed freely and it seemed as if the motorcar was disabled. The Chevalier showed evidence of great annoyance and employed inelegant language.'

De Knyff himself plugged the hole with a piece of cloth. But the incident cost him irredeemable minutes and further dented his confidence of overhauling Jenatzy. Worse was to follow. Minutes later, the veteran was shocked to see that the hare was catching the hounds. Jenatzy skidded into the town while he was still waiting to clear the exit control. It was then that de Knyff acknowledged that his Mercedes opponent could win.

For the first time, Stradbally spectators saw the two top men in their town at the same time. Though unscheduled delays at the controls precluded accurate assessments, they also realised they were witnessing a dramatic turning point. For the second time in the day, Jenatzy was held back a further two minutes at an exit control in order to give his rival a clear start.

Drivers had a momentary reminder of the risks they took as they passed the forlorn debris of Jarrott's car, before sweeping down the Windy Gap descent. Jenatzy's Mercedes was masterful here, the way it held the road. Less so were the precariously wobbling Wintons of Owen and Winton which were still bravely circulating, though now well over two laps behind the frontrunners. As the *Motor* haughtily noted, 'The Americans must learn that they are but as children cutting their eye teeth as compared with men like Mors, Jellinek, Maybach, Panhard and Napier. We hope the Americans will take their lesson to heart and not consider themselves the victims of chance.'

But what the Yanks lacked for in technical expertise, they made up for with courage and Edge-like determination. Winton literally flew across the road and almost overturned, when he smote the pavement on his way into the Kildare control. He then hit a ditch near Simmons Corner, injuring his arm and throwing out his mechanic. The race's oldest driver arrived at Athy driving his overheated machine with one hand. Winton Junior was equally disconsolate, as his father removed grass from the radiator of his wrecked machine. After surveying the damage, the American announced that he would try to coax the machine back to his Timolin base before retiring.

Selwyn Edge was also still in the wars. Motoring's Sisyphus, no sooner was he ever up to speed than another tyre let go and he had to start all over again. His Napier shed tyres twice during this lap and he arrived in Athy with torn and burnt hands and mud-clotted clothes. The delays cost him over 50 minutes. It had been a debilitating eight hours since his elegant and assured morning departure. But he refuelled and headed off without complaining. There was substance to that upper lip.

But there was no stopping the two leaders, who made most of their remarkably trouble-free runs on the drying roads. De Knyff raced towards Athy's Barrow bridge at 3.41, with Jenatzy four minutes behind in hot pursuit. Henry Farman's smile might have brightened race controls, but no levity diluted his racing commitment. Arms akimbo, he was obviously trying in his once more healthy Panhard. Baron de Caters was now the one to have a sudden scare. His Mercedes ran out of fuel just as he left Athy's inward control. Had this happened a few miles earlier, he would have been forced to retire.

Fernand Gabriel enjoyed no such luck, the Mors again frustratingly reverted to its earlier sluggish form. Fuel starvation now lost him over ten minutes and any chance of taking fourth place from the Baron. While the Athy crowd consistently encouraged Selwyn Edge, they had a particular affection for 23-year old Gabriel. 'Sure, he's only a gossoon,' exclaimed a local matron.

*Motoring's Sisyphus — Edge's tyres let go again.*

Up the road at the Moat of Ardscull, spectators eagerly waited to see the progress of the titanic lead battle. The could tell a car's departure from Athy by the distant dust cloud, as well as being able to study its approach along the tramp's heartbreak of a three-mile straight. A *Motor Age* reporter described the view:

> *At the Moat the cars came up the straight line of the road, and then curved in to the right. As soon as you saw the cloud of dust through the trees you caught sight of a small, black low thing rushing along the centre of the ribbon of road stretched out at your feet. As it came along the light yellowish cloud rose right up behind it in a dense, impenetrable mass, showing the little black body up in greater relief.*

> *A mile or so away, you caught sight of two human heads topping the screen in front of the body of the car, and you then began to see that, as they came tearing along, it was with a swaying movement. It would lurch with the dip or rise of the road, to one side, then the other. The greater the speed, the more violently the nose of the machine seemed to sway from side to side. Then you heard the hum, and the tearing thing that was coming on straight for you took shape.*

The Moat's curves also afforded *aficionados* a rare opportunity to observe the competitors' varying cornering techniques. Selwyn Edge took the entrance and exit widely, while the power-sliding Jenatzy regularly shaved the wall with remarkable precision. All agreed that the most reckless seemed to be Foxhall-Keene, which explains why he inevitably strayed over the limit and hit the embankment. A spectator commented 'There was always a sigh of relief when his car passed out sight!' De Caters and Gabriel were reckoned to be smoother than the energetic Farman.

Many drivers passed within one foot of the wall and by the end of the race, the road was badly churned up at the corners' apex points. It was noticeable that while some drivers found time to respond to the enthusiasm of the spectators, Jenatzy rarely moved a muscle of acknowledgement. His eyes were consistently set firmly on the road ahead, his entire concentration focused on his race. 'His features were as passionless and devoid of any expression, save the grim concentration of a statue,' wrote one journalist.

Just before four o'clock, spectators at the Moat saw a dust vortex gather speed from Athy. It heralded the arrival of Rene de Knyff. Then it was eyes back to see where Jenatzy was. And three minutes later, as reliable as a shadow, he raced past in relentless pursuit, as if fully determined and able also to overhaul his French rival on the road. Though it was frustratingly difficult to collate the times, it seemed obvious that the Belgian had consolidated his lead. It was soon confirmed that he had indeed made fastest lap and also restored his margin over de Knyff to ten minutes. He had underlined his race authority and shown the competition that he was equal to any challenge. The Belgian got a big send-off as he left them for the last time.

There was absolutely no performance difference anywhere along the course between the leading cars. Both Mercedes and Panhard appeared equally well matched in speed and cornering ability. It was clearly now all down to a battle between drivers who were as closely akin in experience and ability as they were far apart in temperament. Hitherto, the French had ruled the roads. It was unthinkable that their reign was about to end. But they were now nervously appraising the northern barbarian who was knocking on their once impregnable gate. Competition might eliminate the weakest machine but no matter what Napoleon had said, racing — like revolution — invariably rewarded the hungriest driver.

*Jenatzy hero of Moat audience as he increases his lead.*

There was further excitement three quarters of an hour later when Farman's time was computed. Jenatzy had recorded 61m.32s., two minutes ahead of de Knyff. But Farman's 62m.17s. was a whole minute faster than his veteran team leader. This was sufficient to promote the Young Pretender to second place, half a minute ahead of his compatriot!

Baron de Caters received another ovation as he waved reassuringly to his wife. After the long day, she was relieved to see him start his final circuit at 4.45. Her fellow-grandstand guests assured her 'Now, it is nearly over.' Despite the petrol delay, de Caters had had another fine lap and reinforced his solid fourth place, nine minutes ahead of Gabriel. 'If this is motor racing, I hope we have more of it!', a spectator told Gordon Bennett's representative. Gabriel was the biggest French loser, lapping a whole twelve minutes slower than his opening record circuit.

The only discontented persons were the over-worked motorcycle despatch couriers, some of whom were shabbily treated by snobby English officials. And the journalists who found themselves without the promised Press Steward with whom they were to liaise. 'Yellow was an appropriate colour for his badge,' fumed one London correspondent. Despite a staff of 43 telegraphists, the journalists experienced delays in sending copy — and even more difficulty in obtaining hard news. They occupied an enclosure opposite the timekeepers' area but, lacking the necessary brassard, were not allowed by the police to cross the road. They had to resort to a shouted dialogue with officials.

'A disgrace!' thundered the *Irish Independent* and *Freeman's Journal*, whose correspondents' inadequate source of race progress was a partly obscured and only irregularly updated blackboard which displayed the gross rather than the vital net times. The scribes' legendary rich imaginations had to work even harder than usual. Unlike the racers whose lives were on the line, however, they could always erase their errors. Had they shown a little initiative like Moore Brabazon of Tara, they might have been more successful. A pair of overalls and a pail of water enabled him to go almost anywhere!

LAP TIMES: JENATZY 1H.1M.32S., FARMAN 1H.2M.17S.,
DE KNYFF 1H.3M.39S., DE CATERS 1H.7M.16S., GABRIEL 1H.13M.58S.,
EDGE 1H.55M.21S.

OVERALL TIMES: JENATZY 5H.36M.42S., FARMAN 5H.46M.16S.,
DE KNYFF 5H.46M.50S., DE CATERS 5H.58M.6S., GABRIEL 6H.5M.28S.,
EDGE 7H.56M.20S.

# 17

# Jenatzy Imprints Final Triumphant Groove

Fastest lap underlines leader's mastery — de Knyff repasses Farman — axle failure robs de Caters — Red Devil overcome by reception

## LAP SEVEN (Western Circuit)

The quantity of racers may have been reduced by almost half but the quality and the closeness of the struggle had riveted the attention of spectators. Even a final sharp cold shower failed to dampen the enthusiasm of those who waited in animated anticipation at Ballyshannon, Carlow, Kildare, the Moat, and Athy, for the last stirring glimpse of the intrepid men and their awe-inspiring machines. 'They are slugging it out to the very last mile — like Dan Donnelly and George Cooper!' a Moat spectator remarked, as he recalled the marathon bare-fisted 1815 fight between the local giant and the English champion at nearby Donnelly's Hollow. Mr. Mitchell would certainly have some positive reaction to report to Gordon Bennett.

Onlookers had long earlier picked their individual favourites. The aristocratic Baron de Caters, the boyish-looking Gabriel and the handsome Farman and Foxhall-Keane headed the ladies' lists. But while many respected de Knyff and admired the gritty Selwyn Edge, there was little doubt but that it was the fiery Camille Jenatzy who had really touched lyrical Celtic hearts. French assistance during whatever battle was clearly no match for even older tribal stirrings. Win, lose or draw, Jenatzy's unvarnished daring mirrored that of Cuchulainn and their greatest saga heroes. Like a wild Tipperary hurling cry, 'Come on, Jenatzy!' was a rallying chant now regularly repeated around the 50-mile circuit.

*'Put the kettle on!' De Caters greets his worried wife for final time as he starts the last lap.*

Just after four o'clock, Rene de Knyff picked up his last green card at Kilcullen. He turned westward into the fitful sun of the late afternoon and the fast run to Kildare. The army bugler had not left his post since seven in the morning. Now, nine hours later, his stirring notes brought spectators and householders rushing for their last glimpse of motor racing's bearded patrician. Despite the pressure, de Knyff was again the calmest person in the place. Mechanics rushed around the blue Panhard which they still desperately willed to take the win from Jenatzy. With a final farewell wave, the veteran bounded away from the control.

But no sooner had de Knyff left, than the menacing shadow of his Mercedes pursuer slanted down the hilly hedgerows and into the control at its driver's trademark dispatch. How those Continental tyres served Jenatzy well as he skidded to his final Kildare halt just before 4.30! He permitted himself a wry smile as he savoured the crowd's obvious enthusiasm. But that 'Do not Disturb' sign, all the more tangible for its invisibility, still hung from the side of the hot and travel-stained Mercedes. He was clearly impatient to be off. There had been no such crowds before. And certainly not on those too frequent former occasions, when he had stood alone by the side of a strange road with a broken engine or a wrecked car, and watched his rivals disappear over the horizon leaving only their dust and din to tantalise him.

The aura of race leader had now well settled on him but the Red Devil didn't slacken pace. As was the case all day long, he was a man on a mission. For the final time he raced across the boggy approach to Monasterevin. He occasionally used a hand to shield his eyes from the lowering sun, as he hounded down the ill luck which had thwarted him over the years. As the marsh insects battered against his face and splattered his speeding car, he recalled the fly which had cost him best Mercedes placing in the recent Paris–Madrid. It would be nice to win, all right — like the feeling after breaking those records four years before in Paris. But that had been a lonely unchallenged race against the clock. Today was different — taming these demanding roads and beating the world's best drivers!

But he had come a long way since seven o'clock in the morning and he wasn't going to throw it away on speculation. The race would not be over until he saw that flag. Those still wet sections and hungry culverts demanded total attention. He must stay cool, he must not lose a zillionth of his concentration. He crouched lower and gripped the wheel even harder. Spectators thought that the Belgian had lost his mechanic, Fritz Walker, as he approached at speed apparently alone. But the acrobatic Fritz had hidden himself completely beneath the dashboard to reduce wind resistance and gain further valuable seconds, valuable as in the fur coat award offered by that Dublin store. Jenatzy also had an incentive of which most were unaware. Before the start, Mercedes had promised £5,000 to whoever would win with one of their cars.

Selwyn Edge's mechanic-cousin, Cecil, also had to work for his keep. While Jenatzy's luck held, the Napier duo lost another tyre outside Monasterevin.

Before the end of the lap, a repeat failure cost them over 40 minutes, twice as much time as they had shed on any previous lap. Their once green and pristine Napier was now covered in water-streaked mud which denigrated its sadly mis-titled and fading number one. But Selwyn Edge's courageous persistence gained him almost as many fans as the flying race leader. At every control he was greeted like the warrior he undoubtedly was. A man not given to emotion, he later recalled 'I witnessed enthusiasm at many continental events, but I rarely saw such warmth as was shown to me on the Athy course. It was very encouraging.'

Despite losing their biggest mill to foreign competition, Stradbally's inhabitants had taken a great shine to the continental racers. With many descendants of Huguenot settlers, the town was unashamedly de Knyff territory. Now, as the end of the race approached, the packed streets erupted at the Frenchman's final arrival. 'You can still win!' they encouraged.

De Knyff's urgency as he raced away from the control left no doubt as to his intentions of recovering second place and, if possible, of overhauling the race-leader. But Jenatzy's immediate arrival quickly dispelled those hopes. 'Mercedes will win,' race officials agreed, as Jenatzy spun the car's wheels in his normal uncompromising getaway. Also in a hurry was Gabriel, when he arrived 40 minutes later. Firing on all cylinders, he was on a mission to wrest back a compensatory fourth place from de Caters. A French mechanic had a fright when the Mors brushed against him as Gabriel accelerated away.

Once more, the calmest drivers at Stradbally control were de Caters and Henri Farman. Despite having put 300 miles of hard racing behind them since seven o'clock, they each had time for a smile and a friendly word before heading up Windy Gap for the last time. 'I'm tired, they look as if they are only starting!' said a weary race official. Over at Ballyshannon, Baroness de Caters eagerly awaited the fast-approaching finish of the race she wished her

*'He crouched lower and gripped the steering wheel even harder.'*
The Red Devil and mechanic Walker head for the history books.

husband had not started. After her long wait of ten hours, she was finally beginning to relax. She prepared herself for her husband's arrival.

By this stage, many drivers had lost their headgear. Hatless, the race leader's wispy hair blew around him as he skidded into Athy for the last time at 5.19. He was now less than three minutes behind de Knyff on the road, having made up for all the control delays and most of the 14-minute start difference. But if the Belgian knew that he was on course for the biggest success of his career, he didn't show it. Like Edge, who staggered through to deserved cheers, his face instead displayed the strain of totally committed racing. He gave no indication of over-confidence. As the seconds ticked away, he concentrated on observing the mechanics' final touches for the sprint to the finish line.

Then it was eyes straight ahead, as he hurled the Mercedes down the road towards Ballyshannon. Onlookers watched in admiration and wonder. Their gaze remained on the road, long after he had gone out of sight. They had seen history and they knew it. Nine miles to go! And if Jenatzy and his mechanic were to win, much of the credit would go to that car which hadn't missed a beat all day in the hands of one of racing's most demanding drivers.

Mirroring the improving weather, Gabriel was all bonhomie again as the Mors careered down into Athy three quarters of an hour later, after another trouble-free run. But he also was in no mood to hang about. The delph shook for the final time as the Paris–Madrid winner blasted up the road to take out the last few seconds from de Caters.

*End of a legend — de Knyff on final lap of race and distinguished career.*

The Baron was due eight minutes after Gabriel — how his wife would be relieved to see him. But he never arrived. The minutes ticked by. His supporters were in disbelief that anything could have happened to him so near the finish. A rumour circulated that he had hit a bridge. Then came the news that his back axle had broken two miles outside the town He had managed to contain the skid but his race was over — just 10 miles from home! It was a poor reward for sportsmanship and fine driving. The uninformed Baroness would have her day of worry extended a little longer.

The news hit the Mercedes personnel like a hammer blow. With two of their cars out with broken axles, the Athy-based German mechanics were now concerned that the hard driving Jenatzy might also fall victim to the bumpy circuit. They remembered how Mercedes driver Wilhelm Werner had been lucky not to be added to the Paris–Madrid casualties, when a broken axle had caused his car to overturn. Had their excitement caused them to be careless? Had they missed a tell-tale fracture line during that last urgent stop? But the Belgian had already left them on the final run to the finish. They could only wait helplessly for news from Ballyshannon.

Blissfully ignorant of the Mercedes dramas, all eyes on the grandstand were focused on the road from Athy and the Moat of Ardscull. Race observer Basil Joy took up his position with the Finish flag. Moat spectators would be the first to know whether or not Jenatzy had stayed the course. Water dripped unnoticed from the tall trees in the occasional breeze, as they eagerly scanned the horizon.

As half past five approached, the tenacious Percy Owen completed what was only his fifth eastern circuit lap. His Winton redeemed itself with a time of 65 minutes and 33 seconds, which might have been less, had Owen realised that Jenatzy was once again not too far behind him! Suddenly, in Owen's wake, the expectant crowd saw another rapidly advancing car. As its attendant but rain-diminished dust halo sped closer, a sharp-eyed fan broke the breathless silence: 'It's the Frenchman!' he shouted.

It was indeed de Knyff. Moat enthusiasts waved their hats and programmes as the blue Panhard raced up, braked hard for the first right-hander, then slewed around the left exit and accelerated away towards the finish. Almost immediately from a smaller stand down the road, came a huge surge of applause which sent the wood pigeons soaring. The sustained acclaim which could be heard above the roar of the approaching machine told the crowd that the car — and the race — were Jenatzy's.

The pair disappeared towards Ballyshannon for the final time. They took their last salutes from roadside watchers. Their senses were assailed by the clashing cocktail of oil and summer evening scents. But how pleasant the latter were, compared to the pungency of some of the larger farmyards! The Wicklow hills turned blue in the distance on their right. The slipstream air grew cooler. Ten hours in the driving seat, fatigue would not stay much longer long at bay. Multiple winner de Knyff savoured the final few miles of his long career, Jenatzy anxiously neared his first success. Never had five miles seemed longer. Was that a change of engine note? Was that bump an axle problem or only a pothole? The reliable spire of Fontstown church approached on the racers' left. For seven laps, its timeless aura had reproached their impatient haste. Suddenly, they were past. As they crested the final ascent, they knew they could now practically coast home to the finish and the major placings.

Grandstand glitterati got their first glimpse of the fast-approaching de Knyff. The *Northern Whig* recorded the dramatic finish:

> *Far away a speck was visible with a powerful glass. The signaller stood out on the road under the stand to wave the Finish flag. The speck hurled itself on and on, growing ever larger and larger. Its colour and shape was soon apparent and by the massive figure at the wheel, we knew it was de Knyff. He had fought magnificently to the end. A ringing cheer went up as he hurled beneath the wooden bridge, the car bounding along, plunging like a mad thing. He gracefully lifted his hand from the steering wheel, blew salutations to the crowd, whilst the car kept straight on at speed.*
>
> *He had barely time to slow down when the warning signal rang again. Two minutes later came Jenatzy, well in the middle of the road and running beautifully straight, his body bobbing curiously as the Mercedes plunged over the hillocks. Nothing on the whole course could equal in grandeur, the spectacle of that car rushing under the bridge and the final lap of Camille Jenatzy.*

It was 5.34 when de Knyff crossed the line. As he stopped, he was embraced by a rush of compatriots. Some were moist-eyed as they mobbed the blue Panhard — they had heard that this might be the 39-year old driver's last event. And whether it was or not, he had been trying right to the end. His final lap time was only eleven seconds slower than his previous circuit. Despite his innate caution, the brave gourmet had never been anything less than a racer. 'Farman has slowed!' Panhard personnel told him, as they encouraged his opinion that he had regained second place. But the veteran would have to wait for his compatriot's arrival, before knowing whether he had finished second or third.

*'Well in middle of the road and running beautifully straight' — Jenatzy wins.*

Then the crowd scattered as race-winner Jenatzy roared down on them. His mud-spattered Mercedes was now more slate coloured than white. The Red Devil finished as he had driven, racing up to the stand at unabated speed. He braked at the last minute, to imprint a final triumphant groove on the Irish roads which he already so indelibly scored with his courage and erratic artistry. Ironically, officials then advised him to drive a few yards further, as Basil Joy's Finish flag had been too far ahead of that modest starting post. Abashed at his earlier reservations, car-owner Gray Dinsmore was one of the first to congratulate him.

As the bellowing engine was finally silenced, Jenatzy took time to accustom himself to the sudden quiet. Reluctant to leave the car which had been his trusted companion all day, he nervously surveyed the throng of well-wishers. Deafened by the day-long engine noise, he could hardly hear what they were saying. More used to racing than winning, he was visibly surprised and almost overcome by the warmth of his reception.

But after all his previous career setbacks, none deserved it more than the man whose consistency lay in never failing to try. Defying gravity, the teasing bends, the weather and the best his fellow-competitors could throw at him, he had given his all in what was probably the finest performance of his remarkable career. It was a superb feat of physical endurance, in which vigour, skill and concentration were evenly matched over the gruelling eleven hours since the early-morning start. There was always a day when a man was invincible and this Thursday had been Jenatzy's day. Icarus no longer, he had touched the heavens.

Understandably, it was to be some time before the suddenly subdued Red Devil returned to prosaic earth. He found it hard to comprehend that now, at last, he would have a major trophy to display alongside that stoppered Paris–Madrid fly and the mementoes of previous setbacks. He would be hungry no more. As he was being showered with congratulations, he cautioned others and himself — 'The result will be in doubt until the awards are announced, you know.'

Rene de Knyff also had a long wait until finally, fifteen minutes after Gabriel, Henry Farman raced across the line at 6.30. A quick computation told the veteran that he had regained second place from his team-mate — by a minute and a half! The hapless Farman had had to make a final unscheduled stop for water. It was confirmed that as well as winning the race, Jenatzy had further underlined his superiority by making another fastest lap, a minute and a half ahead of de Knyff and three minutes better than the unlucky Farman. The Red Devil had also increased his race lead to almost twelve minutes. He bettered Selwyn Edge's estimate by four miles per hour to average over 49 mph for the 327 miles, an astonishing triumph over the rainstorm and difficult conditions.

During the day-long race, Jenatzy had been fastest on three circuits. Henry Farman had clearly been the quickest French team member. He had twice made fastest lap and was quicker than de Knyff on five of the seven rounds. Fernand Gabriel and Foxhall-Keene, the only other race leader apart from Jenatzy, had made one fastest lap each.

Twenty minutes after Jenatzy's finish, Selwyn Edge sped past the scene of celebrations to commence his last and loneliest lap. The demise of de Caters rewarded Gabriel with the fourth place for which he had fought so hard, but he was clearly disappointed at not doing better. As Farman finished, Baroness de Caters finally ended her vigil and descended from the grandstand. 'Have you seen my husband?' she enquired. The Panhard driver assured her that the Baron was safe and well and would soon arrive from Athy. The crowd cheered the welcome news.

*Congratulations for racewinner who was reluctant to leave his car.*

Immediately the cars finished the race, each was placed under guard by an observer for a final official check at Ballyshannon House. Mechanics removed the last traces of mud and grease to ensure that there was no extra weight. Just after seven o'clock, the International Commission of the Gordon Bennett Cup officially declared the race over. Camille Jenatzy was confirmed race winner ahead of de Knyff, Farman, Gabriel and the fatigued Edge. Despite his sterling effort, Owen did not complete the seven-lap race distance.

Selwyn Edge had endured no fewer than seven tyre changes, and was later disqualified for having received outside assistance when being pushed out of that control. There was some alarm when Jenatzy was also alleged to have had his bonnet retightened by an outsider, but the Commission swiftly overruled this objection. The close placings of de Knyff and Farman were only confirmed after a thorough re-check of all the control timecards. As the race result was being confirmed, Baron de Caters arrived, smoking a pipe, and was reunited with his relieved wife.

Fifteen minutes later, a car set out with the 'Race Over' card. As it left, spectators were still marvelling at Jenatzy's incredible consistency. On the four western circuit laps, he had recorded times of 1hr.1m.19s., 1hr.1m. 52s., 1hr. 1m.32s., and, finally, 1hr.2m.18s. — a variation of under a minute over 51 demanding miles. For a wild devil, he had been an incredibly controlled one. Charles Jarrott said 'His brilliance was not to be denied, he came through in magnificent style.'

As spectators dispersed, the evening's afterglow reverberated with the wonder of what they had just witnessed. 'By God, it's very quiet again,' a local observed. For many, the noise, speed and drama had provided an unexpected excitement. How docile now seemed the chugging and bleating of the touring cars! The new century suddenly filled with thrilling possibilities. The great race would be discussed around firesides for evenings and years to come. And Tippeenan's Paddy Foley would ever afterwards be known as 'King's Paddy', after dodging security staff to bask in the Lord Lieutenant's brocaded seat.

On the hill outside Stradbally, fans descended on Jarrott's car for souvenirs. Wheel spokes and other parts rapidly disappeared, until a boy took out a sailor's knife and tried to cut off a piece of tyre. It burst with a loud bang and the souvenir ants departed at racing speed. For drivers, spectators, wives and souvenir hunters, Thursday July 2, 1903 had been a rare and eventful day which had touched many emotions.

But as evening drew on, peace and birdsong reclaimed the midlands circuit whose day of drama was already being reported around the world. Tired grandstand bandsmen downed welcome pints. Doctor Ormsby and Sergeant Halley escorted Jarrott and the equally battered Bianchi back to Athy. The returning heroes were driven slowly and painfully along the quiet back roads. The priest travelled with them, frequently administering liquid encouragement from inside his long frock coat. The honeysuckle-scented miles unwound less painfully.

LAP TIMES: Jenatzy 1h.2m.18s., de Knyff 1h.3m.50s.,
Farman 1h.5m.28s., Gabriel 1h.6m.5s., Edge1h.22m.28s.

OVERALL RESULT: 1. Jenatzy 6h.39m.0s. (49.25mph); 2.
de Knyff 6h.50m.40s. (47.85mph); 3. Farman 6h.51m.44s. (47.72mph);
4. Gabriel 7h.11m.33s. (45.33mph); 5. Edge 9h.18m.48s. (35.16mph).

FASTEST LAPS: Eastern circuit, Foxhall-Keene 46m.03s. (52.2mph).
Western circuit, Gabriel 60m.19s. (51.7mph).

# 18 From the Cockpit — Drivers' Stories

Gabriel's frustration — Jellinek's delight — Edge disqualified — Dublin welcomes 'Victorious soldiers returning' — de Knyff announces retirement

Officials and spectators were struck by the camaraderie of the drivers after the race. Tired and semi-deaf from ten hours of constant engine noise, they clung together in a freemasonry of rare shared experience. R.J. Mecredy noted their sporting demeanour. 'There was de Knyff, still in his racing gear, a glow of health on his cheeks and his eyes clean and bright as they had been at seven a.m. He towered above the diminutive Jenatzy, who had not changed his oilskins — and he too looked perfectly fit and hard as nails! Farman was also gay, bright-eyed and unconcerned. Little Gabriel was there too. The winner and losers chaffed each other good-naturedly, and all four exchanged their experiences as if they had been on a picnic, instead of chasing each other like the furies, and risking life at every moment.

*Now, beside the Mercedes, Jenatzy quietly showed them how his tyres had suffered and how stiff the clutch had been. Then, moving to Gabriel's Mors, the rivals followed every little part which had kept it from winning. The Panhards went through the same examination by these sportsmen, who showed not a trace of mean jealousy. Nothing could have been more natural or more pleasing than their friendly conversation, and the words and manners of these men after the race, as they spoke quietly and modestly.*

Through his unofficial interpreter, compatriot Baron de Caters, race winner Jenatzy commented on his success. 'I am pleased most of all for my daughters, who will now be very proud of me! The Mercedes was very good, I am not surprised we won. She travelled with great regularity and was better than the 90 hp cars which had first been entered.

*But it was a very difficult race. I had set my heart on winning, though I had misgivings as soon as I saw the circuit. It is one of the most dangerous and demanding courses I have ever driven on, and not so straight or wide as on the continent. It required great care to negotiate and it was also a severe endurance test for the cars. But I only had one big problem and that was when I was slowed by the American driver. I have never seen a course better managed nor more sporting spectators. Ireland has shown that motor racing can be continued and if for any reason the next Cup is not held in Germany, I would be glad to return and race here again!*

Had there been pit signals in those early days, Rene de Knyff might have had more timely warning of Camille Jenatzy's trouble-free progress. The Frenchman said:

*The course was more difficult than I thought at racing pace, and, unlike the French straights, I was unable to use top speed for more than a few minutes at a stretch. I lost precious minutes taking the wrong road on the opening circuit and again when we broke a water pipe while filling the petrol tank. But I think I really lost because I did not make pace sufficiently fast at the start. I did not want to push my machine too much on such a difficult road, and I imagined that I was making a speed that no one else could be equalling. When I found that the others were excelling me, it was too late. I had made an error in tactics, and I lost through it.*

There was only the hue of exhaustion on the grimy countenance of Selwyn Edge, who finally arrived two hours after fourth-placed Gabriel. He had presented a forlorn sight as he filled up with petrol for the last time at Athy just after seven. He had spent over twelve hours on the road. The remaining spectators applauded his singular spirit. Frustrated after having driven for longer than any other competitor, the Napier driver told reporters:

*It has been an exceedingly bad day for our team. We spent many thousands of pounds in producing the cars which we hoped would keep the Gordon Bennett trophy in this country. Neither time, trouble nor expense had been considered, but all our hopes were shattered by my tyres proving quite inadequate for the work they had to perform, and then the serious accident to Jarrott and the minor one to Stocks.*

Firmly dispelling the stories of punctures, Edge explained:

*Beyond overheating of the engine, I had no mechanical problems. The tyres were simply not strong enough to stand the stress, I won with identical tyres last year but with a slower car. I had yielded to the advice of the manufacturers and had allowed 90 mm tyres to be fitted, in spite of my feelings that the 110 mm covers would be preferable. The car was clearly too fast for the tyres, and they came off at the rims or burst or otherwise went to pieces.*

This was a problem that only high-speed driving revealed. With no practice as for later Grand Prix races, Edge did not find out until it was too late. Without delays totalling almost two and a half hours, the British driver would probably have been up with the race leaders. *Motor News*, however, suggested that Edge lost through over anxiety, having decided at the last moment to use a car 'which had perhaps the most powerful engine in the race — but had only done 50 miles testing.' The Napier dilemma mirrored that of Mercedes over their trusted 60 hp and newer 90 hp machines. Had Jarrott not crashed, when leading Jenatzy, his reliable 60 might have produced a different race result.

Motor racing's perennial 'Ifs and Buts' marked the post-race inquests. Louis Mooers acknowledged that 'American tyres are all right for road use, but they are not built to withstand the terrific strain of rounding curves.' Unhappy with the fuel which had blocked his car's jets, Alexander Winton confirmed that he was taking a sample back home 'to have it analysed and to find out what the Americans have been supplying this country with!' If Henry Farman felt that his substitute water pump had cost him the race, he didn't say.

But there was no hiding the disappointment of Fernand Gabriel who had been confident of a good result. 'The course was by no means difficult, but the car let me down,' he shrugged. The Frenchman must have suffered from nightmares for years subsequently, after discovering the elemental blunder responsible for reducing him to being but a passenger in a potentially race-winning machine. It was caused by the vacuum which developed after his team neglected to ventilate the cork with which they had replaced the fuel tank's original loose cap. 'His car was perfect and we ought to have won the Cup easily,' Mors director, M. Binion confirmed sadly. But winner of the award for the most plaintive complaint was the fervent American supporter who later complained 'The general impression among automobilists is that the foreign element drove too fast for our own people, which is not fair!'

*Unventilated cork cost Gabriel dearly.*

Emil Jellinek's opinions had been resoundingly vindicated by the performance of Jenatzy's car. He lost little time in telegraphing his congratulations to Mercedes — though he typically also found time to refer to 'the scandal of axle breakage.' The management replied fulsomely, saying that the success had healed all wounds between them. Jenatzy reacted to Jellinek's congratulations by doing an uncharacteristic handspring and wiring him 'a thousand thanks!' Also grateful for the Belgian's success was a Kilkenny teacher whom race fans feted in Athy, after mistaking him for the race-winner to whom he bore an uncanny resemblance. Oddly enough, the real Jenatzy was only a few doors away, savouring cigars and wine, after having delayed his departure for Dublin until the following morning.

France's winning of the team prize was a resounding success for the Michelin company. Despite a woefully mis-timed advertisement which rashly proclaimed 'If you want speed, use Dunlop Tyres,' Dunlop did not come well out of the race. Their misjudgement had scuppered Edge's reasonable hopes of retaining the Gordon Bennett Cup. Afterwards, Harvey de Cros climbed Snowdon in an Ariel car which was shod, he claimed, with the same tyres as Edge had used in the Gordon Bennett race. It was a Penningtonian stunt that fell far short of the qualities exemplified by Edge and all the other brave and resourceful Gordon Bennett protagonists.

For the event represented much more than a well deserved success for the daring and hitherto unlucky Red Devil. The Mercedes which had raced for almost seven hours at speeds of up to 80 mph was a triumph of engineering and man's inventive spirit. The race was likewise a success for the exemplary British and Irish organisation, and for the foresight of visionaries like Emil Jellinek and the enthusiastic R.J. Mecredy. The courage, resoluteness and sportsmanship of the participants likewise raised the Irish event from being a mere competition to an inspirational demonstration of the best human qualities.

The *Irish Cyclist* summed up the race's real achievement:

*One thing the Gordon Bennett race did. It showed us that the finest pluck and chivalry, and the most splendid sportsmanship, are still factors in the making of men and that they are not confined to one race or nation. It is hard to know whether to admire most Jenatzy's pluck and nerve, de Caters' chivalrous unselfishness, De Knyff's unfailing good humour, Edge's determined attempt in a hopeless task, the inexhaustible patience of the Americans under repeated misfortunes, or the cool daring of Foxhall-Keene going on with a broken axle. If motor racing did nothing but bring out such qualities as these, it is worth preserving in some shape or form.*

Paying tribute to the RIC race efficiency, an *Autoclub Journal* correspondent commented 'If I were a millionaire, I would offer the Surrey magistrates, and the Chief Constable of the police, a free trip to Ireland to learn their business.' After congratulating race organisers, the *Motor* magazine reiterated:

*The Gordon Bennett race of 1903 was really the first international race in fact as well as in name. Surely, never before has the name of a single individual rushed through the world's printing presses, spread broadcast around the earth, and been scanned by so many millions of readers as the name of Gordon Bennett.*

There were two road fatalities during the Irish race week, each caused by a runaway horse. But apart from Jarrott and Bianchi, the only other recorded race casualties were the two schoolboys. One Kildare lady, however, also claimed to have been a Gordon Bennett Cup victim. Spinster Mary Anne Parnell pleaded after being charged with being drunk and disorderly, 'It was the night of the motor race and it was ginger wine I took to celebrate!' She was fined ten shillings or seven days imprisonment, after the unsporting beak found that she had been disorderly on three previous — and non-motorsport — occasions.

The safe running of the race failed to deprive the inventive Yellow Press of their headlines. One evening organ wrote that Jenatzy had overturned and critically injured his mechanic. The *Evening Standard* whetted readers' appetites with a banner headline 'Franco-German Collision. Several injured.' Also failing to check that Maryboro telegram, the *St. James's Gazette* headlined 'Motor Race Disasters — Cars Smashed!' The Sun screamed 'Big Race Smash!' But the star prize for bold-type misinformation was won handsomely by the special evening edition of the French *l'Auto*. 'De Knyff Wins for France!' it shamelessly proclaimed, and within a short time 93,000 copies were sold to ecstatic French readers. Though a cinematograph club near the Varietes Theatre gave the correct results on its screen, it wasn't until further early morning confirmation that the thousands who thronged the Fauborg Montmartre finally accepted the shocking news of the German win.

In contrast to the previous day, Dublin was almost deserted for most of Thursday. But, stimulated by race accounts and rumours, hundreds congregated around the evening newspaper offices. By nightfall, thousands more thronged the city centre approaches. Villages on the road from Naas were also lined with deferential onlookers. Though he mentioned Camille Jenatzy in *Ulysses*, the writer James Joyce said that his opinion of motor racing mirrored the Persian Shah's reply to King Edward's Ascot invitation 'I know that one horse runs quicker than another, but which particular horse it is doesn't bother me!'

Nevertheless, Joyce's *After the Race* story includes an equivocal account of the welcome which greeted the returning cars on the night of the big race.

*At the crest of the hill at Inchicore, sightseers had gathered in clumps to watch the cars careering homeward, and through this channel of poverty and inaction the Continent sped its wealth and industry. Now and again the clumps of people raised the cheer of the gratefully oppressed. Their sympathy, however, was for the blue cars — the cars of their friends, the French.*

The latter were particularly moved by the crowd's enthusiasm. The *Velo* correspondent wrote:

'Before saying adieu to Ireland, I think we owe to the Emerald Isle our thanks for a cordial welcome from its gallant people. And we will never forget the thrilling welcome of the crowd on our return to Dublin, our carriage going at *walking pace past thousands of people massed on the pavement, and hailing the champions of new locomotion as if they were victorious soldiers returning.*

Some returning motorists, however, complained about one foreigner who passed them at dangerously high speed and without any lights. If they'd only realised it, they could have dined out for years on the story of their lives. Of how, one night on the Naas road, they had seen motor racing history — the great Rene de Knyff enjoying his last-ever burst of speed in a racing Panhard!

*Gold cigarette case for the sporting Baron de Caters.*

Later, at a special Shelbourne Hotel dinner for the drivers, the French veteran and Henry Farman paid fulsome tribute to the race organisers. The Comte de Vogue of the French Automobile Club also insisted 'We will take home with us many lessons in the way a race can be managed, and a course kept and protected.' Sentiments reiterated by Foxhall-Keene who cabled:

*I am sorry not to be with you this evening, but want to tell you how much sincere pleasure it has given me to have been a participant in one of the greatest auto races in the world. Too much praise cannot be given to the wonderful management in policing and taking care of the whole course.*

Baron de Caters had earlier voiced his joy at his rapturous reception all around the circuit.

*The course was bumpier than I expected, but it was a great pleasure to compete here. The organisation worked perfectly and we were never impeded by spectators, whose demeanour was strikingly different to the reckless continentals. I could hear the crowd cheering at all the different controls, I did not expect such a sporting welcome.*

The Belgian was awarded a gold cigarette case for his sportsmanship in stopping to help Jarrott and then relaying news of his accident to race officials. And Ireland would also be forever in his debt for, without his persuasion, there would have been no Gray Dinsmore Mercedes and no Camille Jenatzy competing in Kildare. The Baron's generosity was all the more appreciated when it became known that, ironically, Jarrott had forced him out of the previous year's Circuit des Ardennes event. The English driver had raised such a cloud of dust when he passed him, that de Caters was temporarily blinded and crashed into a stone wall!

Celebrating the success which would swiftly propel Mercedes to the forefront of international motor manufacturing, a guest noted 'Last year, the Germans failed here in their bid to win the International Cup for rowing, but now they have won a prize more valuable to her fame and commerce than a hundred rowing trophies.' Another celebrated the Mercedes achievement by quoting from W.E. Henley's recent poem, which seemed as if it might have been written expressly for the big race:

*Thus the Mercedes*
*Comes, lo!*
*She comes*
*This astonishing dance!*
*This amazing Mercedes,*
*With Speed —*
*Speed in the Fear of the Lord.*

Although a German car had won the race, the French also basked in the glory of their convincing team success for the newly-awarded Montagu Trophy. It was a timely present for President Loubet who was commencing his state visit to London, and a particularly welcome post-Paris–Madrid boost for Panhard. And so reliable were their cars that they were afterwards driven straight to Paris from Le Havre.

But French jubilation was mitigated by Rene de Knyff's confirmation of his retirement from racing. The driver who had dominated so many great long-distance events said:

*No man should race after he has reached the age of twenty three or twenty four and I am almost twice that! The Irish Gordon Bennett is the last motor race I shall ever run. I have been racing for six years and I mean to yield my place to younger men. I have much else to do also.*

Guests rose as one to acclaim the French stalwart and tears flowed freely with the champagne toast. The applause rang around St. Stephen's Green for the man whose name would forever be synonymous with motor racing's fraught pioneering days. Thus was the end of an era confirmed in Dublin's Shelbourne Hotel. An heroic age of fearless drivers, immense roaring machines, dawn race-starts. And giant steps into the unknown, along dusty uncharted roads that led from wooden signposts pointing bravely from Paris to Bordeaux, Rouen, Berlin, Vienna, Madrid.

*End of an era. Rene de Knyff announces his retirement.*

# 19 World Record Broken in Phoenix Park

De Forest's 84 mph — Rolls wins in Cork and Kerry — Edge's appropriate success

Graphic reports of the Gordon Bennett race dominated Friday morning's newspaper headlines. The *Sporting and Dramatic News* leader was typical:

*The British public are only now beginning to realise that a new sport has sprung up in our midst — a sport second to none in its thrilling interest and excitement. One had only to witness the finish between Rene de Knyff and Jenatzy to understand the fascination of the pastime. It was a revelation to see the long low cars coming tearing along like a whirlwind towards the grandstand and spectators at 70 miles an hour. It made the pulses glow, the heartbeats quicken, the breath stand still. Such exhibitions may be condemned as useless and dangerous, but at least they constitute a splendid example of man's courage and nerve, and are a testimony to the skill and brains which have created the modern racing machine.*

An *Evening Herald* cartoon showed two horses gazing over a hedge at a Gordon Bennett car. 'Where are *we* now?' one asked. His companion replied 'Getting left behind!' The publicity gained many new converts, including Dr. Walshe, the Catholic Archbishop of Dublin, who had chanced a lift in a Mercedes when stranded at Kilcullen on raceday. With his dust-laden clerical clothes looking more 'like a miller's suit,' he announced that he was now considering using a car for future pastoral visits!

Hundreds turned out in Athy to see off Camille Jenatzy who smiled broadly at the repeated cheers. After a celebratory photograph with Edge, Jarrott, Winton and Baron de Caters, he set out for Dublin in his race-winning car. Baroness de Caters sat beside him, while her millionaire husband perched perilously on the lower footboard. They were escorted by a procession of motorcars and cyclists. 'Don't forget the speed limit!' the postmistress joked, as she and proud proprietary locals bade him a rousing farewell from the town whose name had that morning accompanied news of his success around the globe.

Dubliners who hadn't stayed up the previous night thronged the display of racing and touring machines at the Earlsfort Terrace ice-rink. The arena glittered with coloured lights. It was a rare opportunity to get such a close look at the revolutionary automobiles. Many were lost in wonder. The music of an attendant military brass band was matched by the loud tattoo on equally melodious car horns. The afternoon's highlight was the arrival of the Gordon Bennett Cup racewinner. Jenatzy was recognised and acclaimed as he arrived via Stephen's Green and a Shelbourne Hotel pit-stop. Another winner was *Motoring Illustrated* magazine which was on sale from early morning with a complete and lavishly illustrated race report.

Charles Jarrott was also royally greeted on his return to the Shelbourne, where he held court despite the pain from his mauling on the roads of Kildare. Overwhelmed with telegrams and letters of congratulations on his escape, he thanked the public on behalf of Bianchi and himself. He reiterated: 'The good wishes from everybody have been a source of considerable consolation to me in one of the biggest disappointments of my life.' But he confessed privately, 'I spent a horrible, painful and sleepless night after the accident. I was in abject despair when I realised that the race was over and that every chance of distinguishing myself had flown. There is no race that I would rather have won.'

Stimulated by racing fever, automobile fans and the Joycean dispossessed took to the streets again on the bright and sunny Saturday morning. The Phoenix Park Speed Trials presented a rare, exciting — and free! — opportunity of seeing their racing heroes and their incredible machines in action in the much-loved city park which had previously served Dubliners well with such tamer activities as cricket, polo and cycle racing. The event would be followed by the Cork and Castlewellan Speed Trials and hill climbs at Ballybannon and Killarney. Hundreds thronged the Nelson's Pillar tram terminus, while others trekked expectantly along the quays in order to arrive for the opening 8.45 a.m. motorcycle race. Newsboys shouted out their headlines from behind imitation driving masks improvised from brown paper. When one of them spotted a white car, he said 'Begorra, they're all getting them painted white to pretend they're Germans that won the Gordon Bennett!'

'The Quality' who packed the special finish area stand were the only ones who had to pay an admission charge. Most spectators enjoyed an equally rewarding view from behind the wooden fences which lined the access paths on either side of the 60 foot-wide main straight. The organisation was thorough, with flag marshals stationed every 200 yards. Their white flags denoted an open road, while red warned of an occupied section. The all-clear signal came from the finish line, by the elevation of white flags in sequence up the track as soon as competitors had exited. Touring cars raced in pairs, while the racing machines competed singly against the clock. Speeding down the slightly sloping straight towards the city, they each covered a 2,583-yards stretch which neatly encompassed both one mile and one kilometre distances. The only hazard was the mid-road Phoenix Monument, whose steps, lamp posts and paving surround were dismantled to minimise the risk. Discerning enthusiasts congregated here, in the confident expectation of a confrontation between ancient history and new.

Newspaper photographs had made the drivers familiar to the public. Rene de Knyff, Fernand Gabriel, Selwyn Edge, and a recovering Charles Jarrott were each loudly cheered on their arrival. The latter continued to lead an eventful life. He narrowly escaped injury when a restive horse crashed into the car in which Mrs. Edge was driving him to Phoenix Park. Drivers new to the spectators included such experienced racers as Frenchmen Leon Thery and Louis Rigolly, Belgium's Baron de Forest and the English duo, Ernest Hutton and Charles Rolls.

*Louis Rigolly's awesome Gobron Brillie sets the tone at Phoenix Park.*

After the motorcycle races, Humber-mounted J.W. Cross opened the car proceedings with fastest time in the 20-heat Touring Car competition of 2 minutes and 6.2 seconds for the 2,853 yards, almost 50 mph. D. Hall's Wolseley took the other main Touring Car event to make an impressive double success for British manufacturers. The Wolseley win was a well-deserved endorsement of the pioneering work of Frederic Wolseley, who had been born only a short distance from the Park. But while the heavy machines impressed spectators as they swerved around the Phoenix Monument, it was the racing cars they most wanted to see. By the time the Lord Lieutenant and his party arrived at noon, the crowd had swollen to over 30,000. An *Irish Times* reporter noted that it had not taken spectators long to familiarise themselves with the finer points of the racing. 'They were soon dogmatising on the various performances, as if they had been for years exponents of the new craze!'

Unlike the Gordon Bennett drivers, most of the Park competitors were neatly attired in very unracing-like suits and ties! Future Gordon Bennett winner, Leon Thery and his Decauville launched the racing car events and averaged 51 mph to beat Arthur Rawlinson in the Light Car class. Then, the heavyweights, de Forest, Rolls and Hutton, battled it out for the Irish Auto Club's Challenge Cup. Rolls looked a likely winner, as his Mors roared away to cover the standing-start mile in 61 seconds. So powerful was the Mors that, as T.C. Moore Brabazon once turned the starting handle, it backfired and sent him hurtling into the crowd! The finishing speed of Rolls's rivals was even faster, however, and Hutton's 1m. 28.6s. seconds for the total distance beat de Forest's Paris–Madrid Mors by one second.

*A special cheer for Selwyn Edge.*

Fernand Gabriel got the biggest reception of the day as he demonstrated his Paris–Madrid winning Mors, the little Breton waving repeatedly in response to the enthusiastic crowd. De Forest, Rolls, Hutton and race veteran Louis Rigolly then lined up for the *Daily Mail* Challenge Cup for the fastest over the flying kilometre. Spectators were spellbound by the noise of the world's most powerful cars, whose speeds soon touched 80 mph. Mere fractions divided the evenly-matched men and machines. Hutton's opening 28.8 seconds was just beaten by Rigolly in his massive Gobron Brillie with 28.4 seconds and then by Rolls, who got down to 28 seconds in a Mercedes. The sensation of the trials, however, was Baron de Forest. His 27.2 seconds was only a whisker outside the 26.8s world record of 83.41 mph.

Spectators cheered when the news was relayed to them. The excitement stimulated further business for the fruit hawkers who, according to *Motoring Illustrated*, were selling 'Motor strawberries at millionaire motor prices.'

Spectators were in for more than a millionaire strawberry treat in the second Flying Kilometre battle for the *Autocar* Challenge Cup. Almost all the cars exceeded 80 mph. While de Forest and Gabriel made last minute adjustments to their cars, Selwyn Edge sped down the straight to record 30.8s. in his new Napier. Hutton beat him by half a second before Rolls recorded another 28 seconds. Then it was the turn of Rigolly, whose 110 hp machine emitted a great sheet of flame as it plunged across the line with another near-record time of 27.2 seconds.

The final competitors were Gabriel and de Forest. The former's streamlined Mors quickly gathered speed after a spectacular take-off. Appearances did not deceive. The park erupted with excitement as he equalled the 83.41 mph world record of 26.8 seconds. All eyes then turned to de Forest, as the Belgian warmed up his identical blue car. His start was just as dashing and the exhaust flamed with each ear-splitting gearchange. Within seconds of leaving the line, he was travelling at a speed never before been achieved by an automobile. The crowd went wild as he flashed across the line in a time of 26.6 seconds. He had beaten the world record at 84.09 mph!

*Baron de Forest starts his world record-breaking 84 mph run.*

With Belgian-born drivers first and second in the Gordon Bennett Cup race and de Forest now on top of the world, the Irish Fortnight had turned into a resounding success for the Low Countries. The prize for bravery, however, went to the Lord Lieutenant's intrepid brother, Cyril Ward. He had volunteered at the last minute to mechanic for de Forest on his record and nerve-breaking run.

The tremendous pace stimulated some of the more staid Automobile Club members to a pitch of fine excitement. They spontaneously arranged two sporting matches to round off the day. De Forest agreed to race Hutton over the complete distance, while friends of Rolls clubbed together for a 30-guineas Cup for a sprint between himself and the ambitious Hutton. *Motor* reported 'Needless to say, when these matches were announced, a burst of cheering broke out from the sporting Irish crowd. No cars of such power had ever before raced side by side.'

Hutton's bonnetless Mercedes was the slower car. But nifty gearchanging secured him an early and lustily acclaimed advantage which he held to the line to beat the Belgian favourite. He then gave Rolls a nervous run for his money. *Autocar* recorded:

> Hutton got away first and led going to the Phoenix Monument, round which he came with a blood-curdling jump and swerve, which slowed him to such an extent that together with the loss of his cap and goggles, although he was a length and a half to the good entering the kilometre, Rolls came by him and won by thirty yards!

Rolls's Mors was the car in which he had set a new world record of 63 mph the previous year. The Gordon Bennett Fortnight had brought no fewer than five world record-breakers to Ireland. They were Jenatzy, Rolls, de Caters, de Forest and Rigolly (who the following year became the first person to break the 100 mph barrier, in his Phoenix Park Gobron-Brillie).

News of the Gordon Bennett Cup and Dublin speed dramas ensured a capacity crowd for the following Tuesday's tests at Newcastle, Co. Down. Hotels were booked out and special trains brought large numbers from Belfast. As they expectantly swung their legs from the conveniently situated stonewalls, Ballybannon hillclimb spectators had a sudden and salutary lesson in the speed and danger of the automobile. With its engine roaring, a French car raced down the hill and scattered officials and spectators as it skidded and swerved, before mounting the pavement. An angry crowd surrounded its driver, Brun, and marshals impounded his Prunel car. Congratulations replaced threats, however, when an interpreter explained that the Frenchman's brakes had failed and only his skilful control had averted death or serious injury.

John Scott Montagu who had steered the Gordon Bennett road-closing bill through Parliament proved equally adroit at the wheel. He was a popular class winner in his Daimler, while Darracq driver Arthur Rawlinson raced up the steep 600-yard hill in just under a minute to win the light racing car category. Once again, however, it was the larger racers which provided the main excitement. Louis Rigolly turned in a rapid 37.6 seconds, which J.W. Stocks quickly equalled. Selwyn Edge's identical speed made it a three-way tie, until Paris–Madrid driver Wilhelm Werner surprised them all with a flying 36 seconds in Jenatzy's battle-scarred but still flighty Mercedes.

A future chauffeur to the German Kaiser, Werner's performance provided a suitable riposte to the German Automobile Club Neanderthals who had denied him a drive in the Gordon Bennett race. But Werner's joy was soon dissipated by Charles Rolls who went two seconds faster. Then, to the crowd's delight, the unfancied Campbell Muir beat them all with the best time of the day, 32.4 seconds. Driving the Mercedes which Alfred Harmsworth had offered to the German Gordon Bennett team, Muir had become a familiar figure during his many days of crafty pre-race practice! While J.W.Cross took the handicap event, Louis Rigolly rounded off the final 2.5 mile Clough speed trial with a 60 mph win from Stocks, whose good run was some compensation for his Gordon Bennett race disappointment.

Ably abetted by mechanic Moore Brabazon of Tara, the lonely, aloof but utterly fearless Charles Rolls garnered most of the concluding Gordon Bennett Irish Fortnight spoils. The sun shone for the Cork Speed Trials at Carrigrohane, where cars shared the road with the open railway track. Private enterprise thrived, as young men gave spectators shoulder rides across the nearby river for twopence a time, and lemonade prices soared with the summer temperatures.

*Rolls and mechanic Moore Brabazon (left) challenge Smith-Cumming at Ballybannon.*

Ernest Hutton made a typically enterprising start in the *Cork Constitution* Cup sprint, before Rolls, his cap characteristically back to front, roared ahead to win in 1m. 49s. for the 2.25 mile distance. Watched by almost 1,000 Kerry people, the future Rolls-Royce co-founder also took the last car event of the Irish Fortnight, the mist-soaked 1,200-yard Ballyfinane Hillclimb on the Tralee–Killarney road. This was despite the sometimes parsimonious Englishman and Moore Brabazon sleeping under the world record-breaking Mors to save money! Moore Brabazon wryly observed 'The droppings of oil and dirt from a racing car during the night do not improve one's early morning appearance.'

The Fortnight concluded with a well-deserved consolation for the tireless Selwyn Edge, whose green Napier-engined craft won the world's first speed-boat event for the Harmsworth Trophy in Cork harbour. Edge's nautical achievement was an appropriate rounding off to the unique sporting and technological event which his sterling 1902 Gordon Bennett success had brought to Ireland. The speedboat course was only a short distance from the spot from which Gordon Bennett had sailed the Atlantic to inaugurate the Americas Cup event.

But the most richly rewarded Gordon Bennett Cup participants were Mercedes and Camille Jenatzy, whose success caused a great surge of pride in Germany and Belgium. A Bosch billboard advertisement soon made his Red Devil features familiar to everyone in Germany. National newspapers unanimously agreed that the Mercedes win had made theirs the leading country in automobile manufacturing. Its Irish victory restored the company's fortunes after the disastrous fire, as well as marking the start of a long and uniquely successful motorsport involvement.

The *Allgemeine Automobil-Zeitung* happily quoted Alfred Harmsworth who had stated 'The nation that wins the Gordon Bennett prize will be the ruler of the international market.' *Automobile Welt* also reminded readers of the other less-sung but equally important national success. 'The German car was superior with reference to tyres, to all the other competing cars, and the Continental Tyres used stood splendidly.'

The Red Devil left Ireland early to see his family, then headed to a celebratory German Automobile Club dinner in Berlin. Mercedes presented him with a new car, which brought his Gordon Bennett winnings to £8,000, a huge sum for the times. Thanks to the unprecedented media coverage, congratulatory letters poured in from all over Europe. They included a guarantee of riches on a higher plane. A religious organisation promised 'Your prospects of Paradise will be greatly enhanced, if you make us a donation from your prize winnings.'

There was little Paradise on earth for many of those around the racecourse, for whom it was business as usual after the departure of the international motoring and media circus. A six-year old child died of a nighttime fit in her locked room at Baltinglass workhouse, while Naas Urban District Councillors were labouring over the form of the Address they would present to King Edward on his forthcoming visit. Magistrate J.P. Doyle was as hard-pressed as ever, sentencing Lizzie Johnston, Kate Hennessy and Molly Lyons to two months each for vagrancy.

But though few of them immediately realised it, the sound of the great racing cars which each of them had heard presaged far-reaching economic and social change. For the spectators it had also been a cathartic experience. The performance of the participants had made an indelible impression, things would never be the same again. The horse and the centuries-old pace would soon be consigned to the history books, and Irish census returns would include a new entry for motorcar drivers and chauffeurs. It was hard to believe that it was only two years since the death of Queen Victoria.

*The Car* magazine summed up their feelings:

*On the minds of the many members of the public who witnessed this epic race, the speed of the cars was the dominant impression. How much more wonderful, however, was the fact that under all the stress and strain of the terrific momentum, the road shocks, the sudden retardation and accelerations, and the perpetual oscillation of the frame, the motors themselves continued to perform their fully rhythmic functions under conditions that no other form of mechanism, from a watch to a railway locomotive, is ever called upon to withstand! To automobilists themselves, half the interest of witnessing a contest like that on Thursday last is centred in the relationship it bears to locomotion generally, rather than the mere incidents of the race itself. That the motorcar is destined to supplant every other form of locomotion but the bicycle, which will survive through its cheapness and portability, becomes daily more assured.*

*Bosch and the Red Devil — pure magic!*

# 20 Farewell to the Titans

Race's rich legacy — Grand Prix replaces Gordon Bennett Cup — drivers' fates — Jenatzy's untimely demise

The last drivers left Ireland, leaving the ghostly monks to resume their peaceful ruminations. The dust and rooks resettled on those midlands roads and princely graves. There was great pride that as well as attracting a major international sporting event, the country had earned the praise and respect of all the players and associations involved. The Gordon Bennett race likewise put the Emerald Isle and its friendly beauty firmly on the visitors' map and marked the start of a rewarding tourist business.

*Motor News* published an enthusiastic leader which advocated the staging of further races in Ireland — for cars powered by alcohol! 'We believe that alcohol has a great future as a motive power and if it can replace petrol, Ireland would benefit immeasurably, for the country is very favourably circumstanced to produce alcohol. The fluid can be obtained from various substances such as potatoes and beet.' The suggestion was not as far fetched as it sounded. Alcohol races had already been staged on the continent — though to the detriment of many engines. Nothing came of the idea, though it was enthusiastically embraced by some journalists — who had, no doubt, had been running on alcohol for years!

But the big race spawned a unique and rewarding motorsport involvement which successfully spanned the following century. This included staging the prestigious Tourist Trophy and Irish Grand Prix series, which attracted such drivers as Tazio Nuvolari, Rudolf Caracciola, Juan Manuel Fangio and Stirling Moss. Also 'Bentley Boys' Tim Birkin, Sammy Davis and Woolf Barnato, and record-breakers Malcolm Campbell, John Cobb and George Eyston. Immortals whose names are spoken of in the same hushed tones as those of Jenatzy and de Knyff. Irish drivers were also to enjoy a disproportionate number of international achievements from Sir Henry Segrave's landmark 200 mph world record to many Formula One Grand Prix successes. John Watson and Eddie Irvine each finished second in the Drivers' World Championship. Unshy Dubliner Eddie Jordan established a successful Formula One team.

The 1903 Gordon Bennett Cup event had simply been an overwhelming triumph. So successful that the *Daily Express* suggested Ireland should be chosen for the 1904 event should Germany feel reluctant to stage it. *Auto Journal* insisted 'Nobody who saw the great race will ever forget it. Ireland was the perfect country to hold it in. Officials, police and the people — all were enthusiastic, intelligent and charming.' There was also amused satisfaction that the spoils had been so diplomatically distributed. Belgian-born drivers finished first and second; the French took the team prize; another Belgian had been awarded a special presentation; a German car had won overall honours. And the Yanks didn't depart empty-handed, as the victorious Mercedes was American-owned. Gordon Bennett's international intentions had been admirably fulfilled!

Apart from its providential boost for the German car industry, the Irish race also marked a milestone in British manufacturing. The event's well-publicised, safe and successful running finally alerted both British public and decision-makers to the automobile's potential. As newspaper leading articles and public commentators lost little time in pointing out that England was being left behind, the first step was the new Motor Car Act which raised the general speed limit to 20 mph and introduced licensing of drivers and registration of cars. While Napier and Wolseley continued their racing programmes, many new manufacturing companies were founded such as Rolls-Royce, Standard and Vauxhall, which in time would make Great Britain a world leader in quality car production.

The success of Mercedes galvanised interest in the Gordon Bennett Cup series. For the 1904 event, Germany was challenged by teams from Austria–Hungary, Belgium, France, Great Britain, Italy and Switzerland. Known as 'the Chronometer' on account of his consistency, Leon Thery overtook the redoubtable Camille Jenatzy on the final lap to take the Cup back to France. He repeated his success the following year, when the 18-driver field included the Irishman Joe Tracy, representing the USA, who was forced out with gear trouble. Thery, who participated in the 1903 Phoenix Park Speed Trials and who died prematurely of tuberculosis in 1909, was the last winner of the famous Cup. It now resides permanently in the French Automobile Club's headquarters on the Place de la Concorde in Paris.

*Gordon Bennett legacy. Tipperary's Henry Segrave broke world land speed record at 200 mph in 1927.*

The 1900–1905 Gordon Bennett Cup competition had become a victim of its own success and the automobile's rapid progress. When it was first presented, the industry was struggling to make its product work at all. But by

1905, motor racing had become too commercial a sport for the series. Manufacturers were severely confined by its strictly national limitations, and the first French Grand Prix of 1906 finally provided them with fairer individual representation.

The Cup perished at the zenith of its powers but it had spanned the early evolution of racing. It had accelerated public interest in motors and motorsport and given manufacturers tremendous impetus in those early uncertain years. With its international status, it also helped to establish a recognised code of signals and regulations and laid the foundation for future motorsport administration. The 1904 German race programme paid an overdue tribute to the founder of the series:

> *The Gordon Bennett race has drawn the nations together on a common sporting ground as no other pastime, industry or interest had ever done before. The competition is not only a splendid encouragement to the automobile artificers of his own Empire, but is a strong incentive to international science and constructive skill.*

*Waterford's Joe Tracy, leading US driver.*

Charles Jarrott in particular regretted the increasing commercialisation of motor racing. He wrote 'I raced at the very beginning of the sport because I loved it. My desire was to race, not to make money. As a business, the motor racing no longer held charms for me. But I will always hold the memory of the long white roads with their never-ending fringe of lofty trees flashing by with dazzling rapidity; the roar and stress of the wind intermingled with the hiss and spit of the engine. I long even now for the possibilities of the past and the living again of all that I went through. It is all gone and finished, but I would not exchange my memories with any man.'

Since the inaugural 1901 Tour, Jarrott had always nurtured a soft spot for Ireland. He concluded:

*Let's have a race in Ireland, so that I may have a reasonable excuse to break away from business ties for a while and go all over the old ground again. And it would be nice to meet again that jovial Irish priest who helped me after my accident — one of the best sportsmen I ever met!*

With the demise of the motor-racing series, Gordon Bennett presented a second trophy for the gentler sport of long-distance balloon racing. Switzerland's Captain P. Armbruster completed his 1921 winning trip of 766 kilometres with an involuntary landing on Dublin's Lambay Island. The *Herald Tribune* proprietor, who visited Ireland only once, donated a final cup for international aviation in 1909. A lifelong bachelor, he stunned Parisian society by marrying at the age of 73 the widow of Baron George de Reuter. He died four days after his seventy-seventh birthday in May, 1918 on the French Riviera, where his name is perpetuated on a *quai* in Menton. Gordon Bennett was almost bankrupt, having spent over forty million dollars on yachts, races, trophies, champagne and general good living. The competition he initiated was immortalised by the French artist Montaut, in a series of stirring art-nouveau tiles which still grace the Michelin House in London's South Kensington. And the 1903 Irish race was similarly recorded for posterity on films made by the British Mutoscope and Biograph Company, the Irish Animated Picture Company, film pioneer Cecil Hepworth and Dublin optician P.C. Cahill.

Two of the Irish Gordon Bennett cars survive. Alexander Winton's car can be seen in Washington's Smithsonian Institute (with some extra gears, it established several US records). Charles Jarrott's restored Napier rubs wheels with Henry Segrave's record-breaking Golden Arrow in Lord Montagu's splendid Beaulieu Motor Museum. Selwyn Edge's 1902 car, which brought the big race to Ireland, is regularly driven in historic rallies by its proud Welsh owner, Johnny Thomas.

Despite road improvements, the 1903 Gordon Bennett Cup course is preserved almost in its entirety, as are the houses where the drivers stayed, including Jenatzy's Leinster Arms and Kilcullen's Bardon's Hotel. A by-pass has fortuitously frozen the sylvan Moat of Ardscull in time. It was enthusiastically remembered by 80-year old Cecil Bianchi, the race's last survivor, when Jarrott's former mechanic visited Kildare for a 1967 commemoration ceremony.

The 1903 race starter, Lindsay Lloyd, went on to become clerk of the course at Britain's first race-track at Brooklands. It was here that Selwyn Edge emerged from his 1907 retirement to set up a 24-hour record of 74.27 mph in 1922. Despite his sterling contribution to British (and Irish) motoring, Edge never recovered from the collapse of his AC car company and he died in comparative poverty in 1940. The 1902 Gordon Bennett victor recalled the pioneering period shortly before his death. 'They were hard days truly, but their hardness and the overcoming of difficulties produced a feeling of triumph which is as hard to appreciate today as it is to describe.'

Charles Jarrott unsuccessfully contested the 1904 Gordon Bennett race and also set a new London–Monte Carlo record of 37 hours. He co-founded the Automobile Association in 1905 and, after many years in the motor trade, he died in 1944. The Chevalier Rene de Knyff kept his Irish retirement promise. For a characteristically well-paced half a century, the all-round Renaissance man was motorsport's most famous and respected international administrator before dying in 1955 at the age of 90. By contrast, 'Foxie' Foxhall-Keene's predilection for bourbon, belles and bacchanalia dissipated his vast fortune. He passed away in a modest cottage in 1941, while not unhappily reminiscing about his sporting youth and the day he set fastest opening lap at Athy.

Just as many drivers had braved the frontier from cycling to motoring, several of the Gordon Bennett participants embraced the equally hazardous uncharted territory of the air. Notably Henry Farman, Baron de Caters, Charles Rolls and Moore Brabazon, who became British Minister of Transport in 1941. Henry Farman retired from racing during practice for the 1905 Gordon Bennett race, having seen the writing when a tree arrested his fall as his car somersaulted to destruction down a gorge. His artistic and speed inclinations soon found free rein in successful aeroplane design and he became one of the most dynamic and far-sighted European pioneers. In 1907, he piloted his Voisin-Farman into the record books with the first cross-country flight in France and he also became the first person to fly a distance of over 100 miles. He died in 1958 and was buried in Passy cemetery in Paris, appropriately close to both Gordon Bennett and the artists Edouard Manet and Berthe Morisot.

*'Weaned on petrol,' Moore Brabazon of Tara became champion aviator and Minister of Transport.*

After setting a new land-speed record of 97.25 mph in 1904, Baron de Caters crowned his racing career with a highly popular home win in the Grand Prix class of the 1907 Circuit des Ardennes. He then became Belgium's first aeronaut and won a major race at Frankfurt Main. He survived until the unchivalrous 1940s, which also sadly saw Fernand Gabriel's premature demise. A 1943 Allied bombing raid on La Garenne near Paris killed the modest man who had won the greatest motor race of all time and made the fastest lap on the western circuit of the Irish Gordon Bennett.

Moore Brabazon of Tara won the circuit des Ardennes motor race in 1907. Turning to flying, he competed many times with Baron de Caters and Henry Farman and in 1909 he won the *Daily Mail* prize for the first mile flight in an English plane. He retired from the race track and the air following the death of his great friend Charles Rolls in a 1910 flying accident at Bournemouth. He entered the British parliament in 1918 and was made Minister of Transport at the start of the second world war. An indefatigable sportsman, he won the Curzon Cup for toboggan racing three times at the Cresta Run, where he had his last run at the age of 72! The great survivor who had abandoned Cambridge classics for mechanics, frequently reiterated 'I always felt very privileged to have been one of the first to have been weaned on petrol and fed on nuts and bolts!'

Few racing mechanics enjoyed as chequered a career as Jenatzy's trusty Fritz Walker, who emigrated to the USA to work for Foxhall-Keene. The pair had a narrow escape in the 1905 Vanderbilt Cup, when their Mercedes overturned and caught fire after hitting a trackside post. The following year, Fritz competed against Jenatzy! He briefly rode with Irishman, Joe Tracy, who set fastest Vanderbilt Cup lap, ahead of Jenatzy who finished fifth. Much in demand for his mechanical expertise, the popular and cheerful Fritz then worked for French champion, Hemery, record-breaker Barney Oldfield and, later, the former air ace, Eddie Rickenbaker. He also participated in the Indianapolis 500 race. But his luck ran out when his driver, Jack Gable, overturned their car in an October 1914 race at Galesburg, Illinois. 'Mercedes Fritz' died of his injuries a few days later.

*Charles Rolls killed in 1910 flying accident.*

A decade after his Irish success, Camille Jenatzy also came to an untimely though not entirely inappropriate end. After retiring from racing in 1910, he devoted himself to developing the Jenatzy Pneumatique tyre company into the largest in Belgium. On a boar hunt in his Ardennes Forest estate in 1913, he decided to play a practical joke by imitating a wild animal. The impression was up to his usual enthusiastic standards. Confusing him for the real thing, a colleague shot him, severing an artery. The 1903 Gordon Bennett Cup winner died while being taken to hospital — fulfilling a prophecy he had once made in his racing days, that he would die in a Mercedes car. He is buried in Brussels' Laeken cemetery.

The men and cars of the Irish Gordon Bennett Cup event marked an heroic chapter in motoring history. Greater than any tribute possible by the most fervent scribe is the stirring firsthand record, penned by none other than Jenatzy himself, of the reality of racing in those days. An account which eloquently conveys the spirit of those fearless pioneers. And — light years from later manicured circuits and pr-packaged drivers — the reality of their world of shifting surfaces and unknown hazards. Mounted high in their virtually suspension-less machines and enveloped in a cacophony of noise, with flailing chains and rudimentary brakes, they raced to the limit without helmets, special suits or any other concession to safety. They were truly the Titans of motorsport.

The Red Devil likened the sensation of racing to being in the centre of a hurricane:

*The car in which you travel seems to leave the ground and hurl itself forward like a projectile ricocheting along the ground. As for the driver, the muscles of his body and neck become rigid in resisting the pressure of the air; his gaze is steadfastly fixed about two hundred yards ahead; his senses are on the alert to detect the slightest abnormal sign.*

*When in the distance a cloud of dust proclaims that another car is being overtaken, a delightful feeling of triumph comes over you. This is the time when you need to recall all that you know of the features of the landscape, for then begins a real journey into darkness.*

*The cloud of dust, at first light, thickens gradually till the only objects which can be distinguished are the treetops on the edge of the road. When you finally emerge, you see the rival car only a few yards ahead, and the dust cloud changes into a trail of flints and pebbles. If the other competitor sees you he will draw aside, but usually he does not heed your signals. There seems to be no room to pass, yet you pass all the same.*

*Death in the wild for the wild Red Devil — the hero of the Irish Gordon Bennett Cup race.*

# Race Entrants, Final Placings and Individual Lap Times

## Gordon Bennett Cup Race Entrants

| Driver | Mechanic | Car | Country |
|---|---|---|---|
| 1. Selwyn Edge | Cecil Edge | Napier | England |
| 2. Rene de Knyff | M. Aristides | Panhard | France |
| 3. Percy Owen | Mr. Graham | Winton | USA |
| 4. Camille Jenatzy | Fritz Walker | Mercedes | Germany |
| 5. Charles Jarrott | Cecil Bianchi | Napier | England |
| 6. Fernand Gabriel | M. Mariage | Mors | France |
| 7. Louis Mooers | W. Starin | Peerless | USA |
| 8. Baron Pierre de Caters | Gustave Girard | Mercedes | Germany |
| 9. J.W. Stocks | Arthur MacDonald | Napier | England |
| 10. Henry Farman | M. Loupi (?) | Panhard | France |
| 11. Alexander Winton | Mr. Armstrong | Winton | USA |
| 12. James Foxhall-Keene | Willy Luttgen | Mercedes | Germany |

## Final Placings and Individual Lap Times

| | Competitor | Car | Lap 1 | Lap 2 | Lap 3 | Lap 4 | Lap 5 | Lap 6 | Lap 7 | Total | Speed |
|---|---|---|---|---|---|---|---|---|---|---|---|
| | | | h. m. s. | h. m. s. | h. m. s. | h. m. s. | h. m. s. | h. m. s. | h. m. s. | h. m. s. | mph |
| 1. | Jenatzy | Mercedes | 48 58 | 1 01 19 | 49 45 | 1 01 52 | 53.16 | 1 01 32 | 1 02 18 | 6 39 00 | 49.25 |
| 2. | de Knyff | Panhard | 49 47 | 1 02 31 | 50 57 | 1 08 16 | 51 40 | 1 03 39 | 1 03 50 | 6 50 40 | 47.85 |
| 3. | Farman | Panhard | 47 31 | 1 10 27 | 49 35 | 1 05 55 | 50 31 | 1 02 17 | 1 05 28 | 6 51 44 | 47.72 |
| 4. | Gabriel | Mors | 53 10 | 1 00 19 | 1 02 37 | 1 04 20 | 51 04 | 1 13 58 | 1 06 05 | 7 11 33 | 45.33 |
| 5. | Edge* | Napier | 46 23 | 1 07 03 | 1 27 59 | 1 24 59 | 1 14 35 | 1 55 21 | 1 22 28 | 9 18 48 | 35.16 |
| | De Caters | Mercedes | 52 17 | 1 08 42 | 51 11 | 1 07 19 | 51 21 | 1 07 16 | | | |
| | Owen | Winton | 56 57 | 1 15 26 | 4 41 24 | 1 19 40 | 1 05 33 | | | | |
| | Winton | Winton | 1 45 24 | 2 34 26 | 1 07 37 | 2 15 36 | | | | | |
| | Foxhall-Keene | Mercedes | 46 03 | 1 24 08 | 51 14 | | | | | | |
| | Mooers | Peerless | 2 01 10 | | | | | | | | |
| | Jarrott | Napier | 48 14 | | | | | | | | |

* Subsequently disqualified

### Fastest Laps

Eastern circuit:   Foxhall-Keene; 46m. 03s. — (52.2 mph)

Western circuit:   Gabriel; 60m. 19s. — (51.7 mph)

# References

Boddy, William, *History of Motor Racing.*
Lord Brabazon of Tara. *The Brabazon Story.*
Court, William, *Power and Glory.*
Du Cros, Sir Arthur, *Wheels of Fortune.*
Davis, Sammy, *Famous British Drivers.*
Edge, Selwyn, *My Motoring Reminiscences.*
Frostick, Michael, *A History of Motors and Motoring.*
Fyffe, Hamilton, *Northcliffe An Intimate Biography*
Georgano, Nick, *Encyclopedia of Motorsport.*
Harding, *The Book of the Car*
Harmsworth, Alfred C., *Motoring and Motor Drivers.*
Helck, Peter, *Great Auto Races.*
Hodges, David etc., *Guinness Car Facts.*
Jarrott, Charles, *Ten years of Motoring and Motor Racing.*
Jellinek-Mercedes, Guy. *My Father Mr. Mercedes.*
Joyce, James, *Dubliners.*
Joyce, James, *Ulysses.*
Laban, Brian, *Winners.*
Lamb, Julia, *Gordon Bennett — the Commodore.*
McMillan, James, *The Dunlop Story.*
Montagu, Lord and Sedgwick, Michael, *Gordon Bennett Races.*
Nixon, St. John Cousins, *Early Motoring.*
Nye, Doug, *Famous Racing Cars.*
O'Connor, Ulick, *Oliver St. John Gogarty.*
O'Donovan, John, *Wheels and Deals.*
Pettifer, Julian and Turner, Nigel, *Automania.*
Posthumus, Cyril and Tremayne, David, *Land Speed Record.*
Rose, Gerald, *Record of Motor Racing.*
Scott-Moncrieff, David, *Three Pointed Star.*
Setright, L.J.K., *The Designers.*
Smith, Cornelius F, *History of the Royal Irish Automobile Club.*
Villard, Henry S, *The Great Road Races.*
Tompkins, Eric, *History of the Pneumatic Tyre.*
Tubbs, D, *Art and the Automobile.*
Young, A.B. Filson, *The Complete Motorist.*

*Autocar*
*Automotor Journal*
*Automobile Club Journal*
*Car Illustrated*
*Irish Cyclist*
*Irish Motor News*
*Irish Wheelman*
*Motor*
*Motor Age*

*Motoring Illustrated*
*Official Guide to the Automobile Fortnight in Ireland*

*Belfast Newsletter*
*Cork Evening Echo*
*Cork Examiner*
*Cork Sentinel*
*Evening Herald*
*Evening Mail*
*Evening Standard*
*Evening Telegraph*
*Freeman's Journal*
*Irish Independent*
*Irish People*
*The Irish Times*

*Cork Weekly News*
*Weekly Freeman and Irish Agriculturist*
*Weekly Northern Whig*

*Drogheda Argus*
*Kildare Observer*
*Leinster Express*
*Leinster Leader*

*Limerick Echo*
*Meath Herald*

*Ireland Illustrated*
*Irish Field Daily Chronicle*
*Irish Tatler & Sketch*
*New Ireland Review*

*Daily Express*
*Daily Graphic*
*Daily Mail*
*Daily Sketch*
*Daily Telegraph*
*Illustrated Sporting and Dramatic News*
*London Illustrated News*
*Morning Post*
*The Times*

*Allgemeine Automobil-Zeitung*
*Automobile Welt*
*L'Auto*
*Petit Parisien*
*Tagblatt (Vienna)*
*Velo Sprint*

# Index

Abbeyleix, 38, 107,
Acheres Park, 61
Adams, Ronnie, 14
Aghnahilly, 71,
Alcohol race, 164
American Automobile Club, 55
Ards circuit, 14,
Aristides, M., 59
Armbruster, Captain A., 167
Armstrong, mechanic, 95, 101
Armstrong, Reg, 14
Ascari, Alberto, 14
Athy, 13, 40, 41, 44–6, 49, 51, 52, 66–8, 70, 72, 74, 82, 86, 87, 95, 97, 98, 105, 106, 109, 110, 114, 115, 119–22, 126, 127, 133, 134, 138, 141, 142, 145, 146, 149, 155, 168
Aucoc, Andre, 34
*L'Auto*, 77, 151
*Autocar*, 53, 66, 78, 86, 90, 91, 116, 159, 160,
Automobile Association, 168
Automobile Club of Great Britain and Ireland, 37, 45, 46, 51, 79
Automobile Club de France, 21, 33, 51, 68, 152, 165
Automobile Club of Germany, 57, 160, 162
*Automobile Club Journal*, 101, 103, 150,
*Automotor Journal*, 92, 127, 165

Bacon, Roger, 19
Ballina (Tipperary), 26
Ballinasloe, 18
Ballitore, 42, 70,
Ballybannon, 156, 160,
Ballybrittas, 71
Ballydavis, 71,
Ballyfinane, Kerry, 161
Ballylynan, 45, 72,
Ballymena, 60,
Ballymoon, 96, 99, 113,
Ballyshannon, 40, 43, 51, 52, 72, 73, 77, 78, 98, 100, 102, 108, 110, 115, 121, 125, 129, 138, 140–2, 145,
Bardon's Hotel, 68, 167
Barnato, Woolf, 164
Barrow, Lorraine, 49
Barrow river, 40, 43, 68, 69, 70, 71, 82,
Barton, Tom, 23
Battle of the Boyne, 42
Bauer, Wilhelm, 53
Beaulieu Motor Museum, 167
Bective Rangers Club, 25
Belfast, 25, 28, 160
*Belfast Telegraph*, 86,

Belgium, 62,
Bennett, James Gordon, 30, 31, 33, 36, 150, 162, 165, 167, 168
Benz, Karl, 19, 20, 21,
Benz cars, 25,
Bianchi, Cecil, 92, 107, 108–110, 146, 150, 156, 167
Bianconi, Carlo, 37
Birkin, Tim, 164
Bonneval, 49
Book of Kells, 13
Borris, 46
Bosch company, 54, 162, 163
Bosch, Robert, 162
Bovril, 23, 78
Brigid, St., 42
British Mutoscope and Biograph Company, 167
Brooklands, 167
Brown, Professor J.S., 25
Bruen, Henry, 99, 113
Brun, E, 160,
Brussels, 169
de Burgh family, 38
Burke, Edmund, 41, 42

Cahill, P.C., 167
Can-Am Championship, 14,
Campbell, Malcolm, 164
Cannstatt, 53, 54, 66, 130,
*Car, The*, 162
*Car Illustrated*, 83, 91,
Carlow, 18, 40, 41, 44–6, 50–2, 70, 74, 88, 96, 97, 113, 114, 119, 126, 138,
Caracciola, Rudolf, 164
Carson, Sir Edward, 39
Castlebar, Races of, 47,
Castledermot, 40, 41, 45, 51, 52, 70, 96, 97, 113, 128,
Castlewellan, 39, 156,
De Caters, Baron Pierre, 13, 18, 50, 53, 54, 57, 61, 68, 76, 83, 89, 91, 93, 102, 108, 110, 111, 114, 115, 117, 122, 124, 127, 129,130, 134–6, 138, 140–2, 145–7, 150, 152, 153, 155, 160, 168
De Caters, Baroness Axeline, 87, 94,102, 119, 129, 136, 138, 140–42, 145, 146, 155
Chamberlain, Col. Neville, 88
Chanteloup, 61
Charlemagne, 64
Charron, Fernand, 21, 30, 34, 35, 59,
Chicago, 22, 28, 59,
Circuit des Ardennes, 38, 58, 61, 62, 64, 94, 102, 153, 168
Circuit de Sud-East, 59

Circuit du Nord, 28, 61,
Cleveland, 59
Clonmel, Lady, 23
Clough, 161
Cobb, John, 164
Cobh, 33
Coleman, Pembroke, 51
Colohan, Dr. John, 25, 26
Continental tyres, 56, 76, 86, 129, 139,
Cooney, John C., 24, 26
Cork, 37, 39, 79, 82, 131, 156, 161
Cork Grammar School, 25
de Crawhez, Baron, 57, 64,
Crean, Henrietta Agnes, 33
Cresta Run, 169
Cromwell, Oliver, 41,
Curragh, 13, 26, 40, 42, 68, 88, 131,
De Cros, George, 28, 61, 64,
Du Cros family, 25, 64
Du Cros, Harvey, 18, 25, 27, 64, 129, 150,
Cross, J.W., 157, 161
Curragh, 11, 14, 45, 71, 73, 78, 104, 105, 119,

*Daily Express*, 21, 83, 165
*Daily Mail*, 18, 21, 33, 100, 158, 168
Daimler cars, 53, 54
Daimler, Gottlieb, 19, 21,
Daimler, Paul 53
Dashwood Hill, 55
Davis, Sammy, 121, 164
Daytona, 59
De Dion Bouton, 21
De Dion, Marquis, 29
Deasy. H.H., 37
Derry, 60
Devlin, Joseph, 69
Dinsmore, Clarence Gray, 53, 68, 91, 94, 144, 153
Dobbs, Joseph, 107
Donegal, 37
Donnelly, Dan, 138
Donnelly's Hollow, 109, 138,
Dublin, 18, 22, 23, 25, 37–40, 64–9, 74, 79, 83, 85, 139, 151, 155, 156, 167
*Dubliners*, 24, 151
Dufferin, Lady, 23
Dunamase, Rock of, 41, 69, 71, 73, 86, 107, 132,
Dundrod circuit, 11, 14
Dunlavin, 38
Dunlop, Joey, 14
Dunlop, John Boyd, 18, 24, 25,
Dunlop tyres, 56, 86, 90, 93, 129, 150,

# Index

Edge, Cecil, 90, 106, 139,
Edge, Selwyn, 11, 13, 18, 21, 22, 30, 35–8, 45, 49, 55, 57, 59–61, 63, 69, 72, 77, 83, 84, 86, 90, 93, 95–8, 100, 102–7, 109–14, 117, 119, 120, 122, 124, 129, 130, 133–5, 138–41, 144, 145, 148–50, 155, 157, 159–61, 167,
Edgeworth, Richard L., 25
Edward VII, King, 22, 150, 151, 162
Ellis, Hon. Evelyn, 22
Emancipation Day Run, 22
Empire Theatre, 74
*Erin* coat, 74
*Evening Herald*, 17, 85, 155,
*Evening Mail*, 46, 85,
*Evening Telegraph*,
Eyston, George, 164

Fairyhouse, 38
Fangio, Juan Manuel, 14, 164
Farman, Henry, 47, 54, 57, 58, 69, 76, 77, 83, 94, 97, 102, 103, 105, 110, 111, 113, 114, 117, 121, 124, 126, 127, 129–31, 133–6, 138, 140, 143–5, 147, 152, 168
Farman, Maurice, 57, 64
*Ferdinand de Lesseps* ship, 64, 65, 67,
Fingleton's farm, 108
Foley, Paddy, 146
Fontstown, 70, 73, 142
Ford, Henry, 18, 26, 28, 37, 59, 95,
de Forest, Baron, 64, 157, 158, 159, 160,
Fournier, Henri, 32, 35, 54
Foxhall-Keene, James, 18, 53, 57, 61, 68, 76, 89, 95, 97, 100, 102, 103, 109, 111, 113, 114, 117, 118, 135, 138, 145, 150, 152, 168
Frankfurt Main, 168
*Freeman's Journal*, 25, 26, 49, 50, 79,
French, Percy, 69,

Gable, Jack, 169
Gabriel, Fernand, 11, 13, 42, 43, 49, 54, 58, 61, 62, 64, 65, 68, 72, 75, 83, 89, 92, 93, 98, 102, 105, 108–111, 113, 114, 117, 121–4, 127–9, 132, 134–6, 138, 140, 141, 144, 145, 147–9, 156, 158, 159, 168
Galway, 82
Gauguin, Paul, 37, 73
Gillie, M.H., 25
Giradot, Leonce, 35, 36
Girard, Gustave, 61, 93,
Glasgow, 59,
Goff, Sir William, 38, 77
Gogarty, Oliver St.John, 26
Goldsmith, Oliver, 19
Goodridge Clipper tyres, 56
Gordon Bennett Cup, 18, 34, 36, 37, 103, 114, 129, 132, 150, 156,
Gordon Bennett races, 11, 13, 17, 23, 25, 28, 29, 32, 36–8, 40, 54, 57, 59, 60, 66, 100, 150, 153, 155, 165, 166, 168
Grahame-White, Claud, 35
Griese river, 43
Grosse Point, 28, 59,

Grosvenor Hotel, 68
Guinness brewers, 25
Guinness, Algy Lee, 14
Guinness, Bill Lee, 14

Hall, D, 157
Halley, Sergeant, 107, 108, 146
Halverstown, 70,
Hamilton, Hugh, 14
Harkness, Harry, 55
Harmsworth, Lord Alfred, 18, 26, 33, 53, 160,
Harvey, Rev. Ralph, 25
Hawthorn, Mike, 14
Healy, Tim, 39
Hearst, William R., 33
Hemery Victor, 169
Henley, W.E., 153
Hepworth, Cecil, 167
Hieronymous, Otto, 57, 61
High Cross of Moone, 43
Hopkirk, Paddy, 14
Humbert, General, 48
Hume, Willie, 25,
Hutton, Ernest, 157, 158, 159, 160, 161,

Indianapolis 500, 169
Inglis, J.J., 75
*Irish Cyclist*, 14, 66, 79, 150,
*Irish Field*, 12, 37, 73, 79, 104,
Irish Grand Prix, 164
*Irish Independent*, 83, 137,
*Irish Wheelman*, 19, 22, 120,
Irvine, Eddie, 14, 164
Iveagh, Lord, 25, 26

Jarrott, Charles, 14, 15, 26–8, 34, 41, 45, 48, 55, 58–63, 69, 72, 83, 84, 88, 90–2, 97, 101–3, 105, 107–10, 113, 114, 133, 146, 150, 152, 153, 155–7, 166–8
Jellinek, Emil, 35, 53, 61, 133, 149, 150,
Jellinek, Mercedes, 53
Jenatzy, Camille (The Red Devil), 11, 13, 18, 21, 35, 54, 57, 58, 62, 68, 72, 76, 77, 82, 83, 91, 94, 97, 98, 100–106, 109–14, 117, 118, 121–5, 129–36, 138, 140–51, 153, 155, 156, 160, 162–4, 167, 169, 170
Johnson, Amy, 81
Johnson, Claude, 37, 39,
Jordan, Eddie, 164
Joy, Basil, 142, 144
Joyce, James, 12, 20, 24, 32, 55, 151,

Kells, 26
Kenealy, Arabella, 74
Kennedy, Dr. Ben, 109
Kerry, 26, 39, 156,
Kilbeggan, 38
Kilcullen, 38, 40, 41, 44, 45, 51, 52, 68, 70, 71, 74, 77, 88, 96, 100, 104, 112, 113, 117, 118, 121, 125, 127, 129, 139, 155, 167
Kildare, 38, 39, 40, 42, 46, 47, 51, 52, 56, 65, 66, 71, 72, 77, 86, 104, 105, 119, 122, 131, 132, 133, 138, 139, 151, 153, 156, 167

*Kildare Observer*, 75, 82,
Kilkenny, 26, 39, 149
Killaloe, 26
Kilmeade, 67,
Kipling, Rudyard, 18
Kirkistown circuit, 14
De Knyff, Rene, 11, 13, 18, 30, 35, 36, 46, 54, 57–9, 62, 69, 77, 83, 88, 90, 91, 94, 96, 97, 98, 100, 103, 106, 107, 110–14, 117, 118, 121–5, 128–36, 138–45, 147, 148, 150–5, 157, 164, 168

Lambay Island, 167
Lane, Hugh, 24
Langrishe, Hercules, 27
Large, Harry, 68
Lautrec, Toulouse, 20
Leadbetter, Mary, 68
Leger, Ferdinand, 19
Lehmann, Charley, 53, 116,
Leinster Arms Hotel, 68, 106, 167,
*Leinster Leader*, 74, 79,
Leo XIII, Pope, 37
Levassor, Emile, 30
Light Locomotives (Ireland) Act, 39
Limerick, 26, 82
Lisle, Joseph, 55, 88
Livingstone, David, 33
Lloyd, Col Lindsay, 89, 90, 92, 95, 167
London, 22, 37,
London, Jack, 37
Long Island, 59,
Loubet, President, 153
Luttgen, Willy, 68, 95, 109, 115, 117, 118,

McCormack, John, 74
MacDonald, Arthur, 99
Maganey, 50, 70,
Magrath, Col. John, 26
Manet, Edouard, 168
Mariage, M., 58, 102, 127, 128, 132,
Mary, Queen, 42
Maryboro (Portlaoise), 38, 40, 42, 71, 86, 105, 120, 122,
Matheson, C.W., 55
*Matin*, 46
May, Caroline, 33
Maybach, Wilhelm, 20, 53, 133,
Mayhew, Mark, 112
Mecredy, R.J., 18, 22, 26, 37, 43, 52, 67, 147, 150,
Menzel, Carl, 128
Mercedes cars, 35, 53, 54, 72, 76, 101, 114, 117, 118, 121, 123, 126, 129–31, 133–5, 139–41, 144, 147, 149, 150, 153, 155, 158, 160, 165, 169
Michelin, Andre, 64, 93
Michelin, Edouard, 30,
Michelin tyres, 56, 76, 129, 150, 167
Mille Miglia, 11
Mitchell, Mr., 116, 138
Monasterevin 40, 47, 51, 52, 71, 104, 105, 122, 139,
Moat of Ardscull, 13, 41, 66, 67, 70, 83, 86, 88, 102, 110, 119, 120, 122, 126, 134, 135, 142, 167

Mondello Park circuit, 14
Montagu, Hon. John Scott, 38, 160,
Montagu of Beaulieu, Lord, 167
Montagu trophy, 153
Montaut, 49, 167
Monte Carlo Rally, 14
Montreaux, 37
Mooers, Louis, 55, 56, 59, 60, 65, 68, 69, 77, 83, 89, 93, 99, 102, 105, 109, 115, 116, 124, 149,
Moone, 40, 68, 70, 112,
Moore, George, 19
Moore-Brabazon, T.C., 32, 128, 137, 158, 161, 168, 169
Morgan, Ronan, 14
Morisot, Berthe, 168
*Morning Post*, 63,
Mors cars, 42, 52, 54, 55, 61, 64, 65, 75, 102, 105, 109, 111, 114, 123, 127, 129, 132, 134, 141, 147, 158, 160,
Mors, Emile, 54, 64, 133,
Moss, Stirling, 11,14, 164
*The Motor*, 78, 97, 133, 150, 159,
*Motor Age*, 134,
*Motor News*, 18, 37, 52, 125, 128, 149, 164,
*Motoring Illustrated*, 37, 43, 44, 156, 158,
Mountmellick, 43
Muir, Campbell, 160
Murphy, William Agnew, 77

Naas, 38, 41, 65, 75, 79, 86, 151, 152,
Nannetti, J.P., 23
Napier cars, 35, 36, 55, 56, 60, 72, 76, 77, 90, 97, 100, 106, 107, 112, 117, 129, 133, 140, 149, 159, 165, 167
Napier, David, 60, 133,
Napier, Montagu, 79,
Navan, 26
Newbridge, 40, 78, 86,
*New Ireland Review*, 41
New York, 33, 59, 61, 78,
*New York Herald Tribune*, 33, 34, 167
Nice, 37, 53, 54, 59, 61,
Nice–Marseilles–Nice race, 59,
Nixon, Willie, 28, 48, 49
Norman, Henry JP, 89,
*Northern Whig*, 39, 40, 143,
Nurburgring circuit, 14
Nuvolari, Tazio, 14, 164

O'Connor, Jerry, 28
O'Connor, Roderic, 73
Oldfield, Barney, 169
O'Meara, Frank, 41
Ormsby, Dr. Lambert, 109, 146
Owen, Percy, 46, 55, 56, 59, 60, 68, 76, 86, 90, 91, 97, 98, 100, 101, 102, 109, 115, 127, 129, 133, 142,

*Pall Mall Gazette*, 40,
Panhard, A., 64
Panhard cars, 30, 34, 52, 54, 55, 56, 58, 64, 76, 77, 97, 107,123, 129, 130, 133, 134, 135, 139, 142, 143, 147, 152, 153,
Panhard-Levassor 21, 22, 58,
Paris, 33, 54, 57, 58, 61, 66, 78, 139, 151, 153, 154, 165, 168

Paris–Amsterdam–Paris race, 30
Paris–Berlin race, 34, 54, 61,
Paris–Bordeaux race, 30, 33, 35, 54, 59, 60,
Paris–Innsbruck race, 18, 35
Paris–Lyon race, 35,
Paris–Madrid race, 11, 13, 17, 28, 32, 36, 46, 48–50, 54, 57, 58, 61–4, 82, 89, 92, 94, 106, 112, 139, 142, 153,
Paris–Rouen reliability trial, 21, 34,
Paris–St. Malo race, 62
Paris–Trouville race, 30
Paris–Vienna race, 38, 57, 60, 61, 89, 129,
Parnell, Charles Stewart, 26
Parnell, Mary Anne, 151
Pau circuit, 59,
Phoenix Park, 14, 17,
Peare, Bill, 38
Peerless, 55, 56, 59, 77, 93, 99, 115, 116,
Pennington, Joel, 22
Percy, James C., 43, 67,
*Petit Parisien*, 46
Philip, King of Spain, 42
Phillips, Capt. Robert, 51,
Phoenix Park, 23, 39, 63, 79,
Phoenix Park Speed Trials, 156–160, 165
Plunkett, Horace, 26, 79,
Porter, Leslie, 28, 49
Prade, George, 77
Ptolemy, 41,
Punchestown, 38

Queen's County Council, 39

Rawlinson, Arthur, 158, 160,
Redmond, John, MP, 39
Renoir, Auguste, 19
Renault, Marcel, 49, 57
de Reuter, Baroness, 167
Rickenbacker, Eddie, 169
Rigolly, Louis, 64, 157, 158, 159, 160, 161
Roberts, Field Marshal, 77
Roe, Michael, 14
Rolls, Charles, 21, 27, 45, 55, 57, 60, 157, 158, 159, 160, 161, 168, 169
Rolls-Royce, 21, 27, 165
de Rothschild, Baron, 17, 58, 64, 90,
Royal Irish Automobile Club, 26
Royal Irish Constabulary, 47, 52, 68, 75, 88, 101, 115, 128, 150,
Russellstown, 70, 73

*St. James's Gazette*, 151
Salleron, Jean, 61, 64, 65, 83,
Salmon, Head Constable, 75
Sampson, Lyons, 75
Scottish Automobile Club, 79
Segrave, Henry, 116, 164, 167
Shackleton, Ernest, 42
Shelbourne Hotel, 79, 152, 154, 156,
Simmons cross, 72, 105, 133,
Smith, Rosemary, 14
Smith-Cumming, Lt. Mansfield, 88,
Smithsonian Institute, 167
Spa–Bastogne–Spa race, 59,
*Sporting and Dramatic News*, 155
*Standard*, London, 57, 151,

Stanley, Henry Morton, 33
Starin, W., 93
Stocks, W.S., 55, 60, 63, 69, 77, 86, 94, 99, 107, 113, 114, 119, 160, 161
Stradbally, 40, 51, 52, 71, 107, 109, 110, 132, 133, 140, 146,
*The Sun*, 151
Swindley, Harry, 110

Tampier, V., 51, 75, 89,
*The Irish People*, 47, 69,
*The Irish Times*, 39, 67, 73, 133, 157,
*The Times*, 116
Theatre Royal, 74
Thery, Leon, 64, 157, 158, 165
Thomas, Johnny, 167
Thomastown, 73, 101
Timolin, 38, 40, 68, 70, 133,
Tippeenan, 40, 73, 87, 146,
Tipperary, 14, 138
Tivoli Theatre, 74, 99
Tour de France, 58, 59,
Tour of Great Britain, 1,000-miles, 27
Tour of Ireland, 1000-miles, 26
Tourist Trophy races, 11, 164
Tracy, Joe, 28, 165, 166, 169.
Tullamore, 38
La Turbie, 48, 53, 54, 58,

*Ulysses*, 24, 151

Vanderbilt Cup races, 118, 169.
*Velo*, 151
Voisin-Farman, 168

Wakefield trophy, 11,
De Walden, Lord Howard, 22
Walker, Fritz, 62, 101, 139, 169.
Walshe, Archbishop, 155
Ward, Cyril, 159
Warden, John B., 64
Wards, The, 38
Waterford, 26, 28, 37, 79, 166
Watson, Cathcart, MP, 39
Watson, John, 14, 164
Welbeck, 55,
Werner, Wilhelm, 57, 142, 160
Westmeath County Council, 39
Westrumite, 46, 88, 102
Wexford, 26
Windy Gap, 40, 71, 90, 132, 133, 140,
Winton, Alexander, 34, 35, 55, 57, 59, 60, 68, 78, 86, 95, 101, 109, 115, 122, 124, 127, 129, 133, 149, 155,167,
Winton cars, 55, 56, 59, 65, 91, 127, 133, 142, 167,
Wolseley cars, 35, 49, 55, 157, 165
Wolseley, Frederick York, 18, 157,
Woods, Stanley, 14
Wollen, T.H., 51
Wright brothers, 37
Wyndham, George, 40
Wyndham Land Act, 24, 72, 77

Yeats, John B., 24
Yorkshire Automobile Club, 83
Young, A.B.Filson, 18

Zborowski, Count Eliot, 35, 38, 48, 58,
De Zuylen de Nyevelt, Baron, 64